D0812803

"Big Bang, Big God *is an engaging introductory account of the history of Big Bang Cosmology, including a detailed discussion of the underlying physics and a Christian perspective on its theological and philosophical implications. Holder explains why fundamental questions such as "Why is there something rather than nothing?" are not answerable within science, and he is rightly critical of the multiverse idea when it is invoked to account for the fine-tuning of the universe without the need for a Creator. I warmly commend this carefully argued monograph as a most valuable resource for anyone wishing to engage in the conversation between modern science and Christian faith, and who is also looking for arguments supporting the case that belief in God is reasonable."*

John Pilbrow, Emeritus Professor of Physics, Monash University, and former President of ISCAST (Institute for the Study of Christianity in an Age of Science and Technology)

"Are 'many universes' a satisfactory alternative to belief in one Creator? With lucid rationality, this fine book guides the reader deftly through some of the most profound questions in contemporary science."

Roger Trigg, Emeritus Professor of Philosophy, University of Warwick, and Senior Research Fellow, Ian Ramsey Centre, Oxford

"Rodney Holder combines expertise in both science and theology to explore the exciting question of the origin of the universe – he does so in a way that reflects the importance, complexity and fun of these big questions."

Revd Professor David Wilkinson, Principal, St John's College, Durham University

BIG BANG, BIG GOD:

A UNIVERSE DESIGNED FOR LIFE?

RODNEY D. HOLDER

LION

Published by Lion Books
an imprint of
Lion Hudson plc
Wilkinson House, Jordan Hill Road,
Oxford OX2 8DR, England
www.lionhudson.com/lion

ISBN 978 0 7459 5626 8
e-ISBN 978 0 7459 5786 9

First edition 2013

Picture Acknowledgments

Cover images: background © Victor
Habbick Visions/Science Photo Library/
Corbis; seedling © Ingimage.com
p. 16, figure 1.3 © NASA's Imagine the
Universe. Used by permission
p. 17, figure 1.5 © The Art Archive/
Mondadori Portfolio
p. 50, figure 2.2 © TopFoto
p. 72, figure 4.1 © iStockphoto

Text Acknowledgments

Every effort has been made to trace the
original copyright holders where required.
In some cases this has proved impossible.
We shall be happy to correct any such
omissions in future editions.

Scripture quotations are from The Revised
Standard Version of the Bible copyright
© 1946, 1952, 1957, 1971 and 1973 by
the Division of Christian Education of the
National Council of Churches of Christ
in the United States of America. Used by
permission. All Rights Reserved.

pp. 19, 100, 105, 166: Quotes attributed
to Albert Einstein used by permission of
the Albert Einstein Archives, The Hebrew
University of Jerusalem.

p. 28: Extract from *Mr Tompkins in Paperback*
by George Gamow © Cambridge University
Press, 2012, reproduced with permission.

pp. 33–34, 37: Extracts from *Religion and
the Scientists* by Fred Hoyle, SCM Press
1959 © SCM Press. Used by permission of
Hymns Ancient & Modern Ltd.

p. 37: Extract from "The Universe: Past
and Present Reflections" by Fred Hoyle in
Engineering and Science Magazine © 1981.
Used by permission of *Engineering and
Science Magazine*.

pp. 40–42: Extracts from *Cosmology and
Controversy* by Helge Kragh © 1996
Princeton University Press. Reprinted by
permission of Princeton University Press.

p. 60: Extracts from *A Brief History of Time:
From the Big Bang to Black Holes* by Stephen
Hawking, published by Bantam Press.
Reprinted by permission of The Random
House Group Limited.

pp. 75, 76: Extracts from *Letters and Papers
from Prison*, The Enlarged Edition by
Dietrich Bonhoeffer, SCM Press 1971 ©
SCM Press. Used by permission of Hymns
Ancient & Modern Ltd.

The author is grateful to the publishers
of the following for permission to utilise
material from his earlier academic work:
Rodney D. Holder, *God, the Multiverse,
and Everything* (Farnham: Ashgate, 2004)
© 2004. Used by permission of Ashgate
Publishing.

Rodney D. Holder, "Georges Lemaître and
Fred Hoyle: Contrasting Characters in Science
and Religion", in *Georges Lemaître: Life,
Science and Legacy*, ed. Rodney D. Holder
and Simon Mitton (Heidelberg: Springer,
2012), pp. 39–53. Used by permission of
Springer Science+Business Media.

Rodney D. Holder, "God and the Multiverse:
A Response to Stephen Hawking", *Faith
and Thought* 51 (2011), 3–17. Used by
permission of *Faith and Thought*.

A catalogue record for this book is available
from the British Library

Printed and bound in the UK, August
2013, LH26

For Shirley,
with love

CONTENTS

FOREWORD

Questions of origin have always fascinated people, and those with this concern will find much of interest in this book. One of the outstanding achievements of twentieth-century science was the establishment of the Big Bang theory of cosmology. The universe that we observe today has been shown to have a finite history, stemming from an originating event (the Big Bang) some 13.8 billion years ago.[1] Initially the cosmos was very simple, an almost uniform expanding ball of energy, but over its long history it has become richly complex, with the human brain being the most complicated consequence of that evolving process of which we are aware. Many of the processes by which this complexity came to birth are well understood, and the surprising conclusion has emerged that they were only possible because the fundamental laws of nature operating in our world take a very precise, "finely-tuned", form. Small variations in the strengths of the basic forces of nature would have rendered the development of carbon-based life impossible.

These are very remarkable scientific discoveries, and Rodney Holder gives a clear and detailed account of how they arose from a combination of deep theoretical understanding and exquisitely precise astronomical observations. He tells a remarkable scientific story, which is of the highest interest in its own right, but its character is such that it almost inevitably raises metascientific questions of whether there is also meaning and purpose to be discerned in this subtle and fertile process. Is the fine-tuning of our universe for carbon-based life a sign that the will and purpose of a divine Creator lies behind its history? Or is it a sign that our universe is just one member of a vast array of different universes (a multiverse), with ours simply by chance the one with a winning ticket for life in a gigantic multiversal lottery? Rodney Holder gives a careful and fair-minded discussion of these metascientific issues, drawing on insights from philosophy and theology.

Scientific discovery is one of the most impressive achievements of human culture. This book will give its readers ready access to the understanding and evaluation of issues of deep significance arising from one result of that great endeavour.

John Polkinghorne
Cambridge, UK

THE BIG BANG: HISTORY OF A SCIENTIFIC THEORY

> The evolution of the world can be compared to a display of fireworks that has just ended: some few red wisps, ashes and smoke. Standing on a well-chilled cinder, we see the slow fading of the suns, and try to recall the vanished brilliance of the origin of the worlds.
>
> **Georges Lemaître (1950)**[1]

The Beginnings of Modern Cosmology

Did the universe have a beginning in time or has it always existed? What were the conditions that enabled life to develop in the universe? Is the universe finite or infinite in extent? Does it always stay the same or is it changing over time? These are fundamental questions but in order to answer them we first need to take a step back in history, because our perspective on these issues has changed completely since the beginning of the twentieth century.

The 25th of November 1915 was a momentous day in the annals of science and in the whole history of human intellectual endeavour. This was the day on which Albert Einstein presented to the Prussian Academy of Sciences a new theory of gravity that would supersede the theory of Newton. Einstein called his breakthrough the "general theory of relativity".

Newton had pictured space as an infinite container in which massive bodies attracted each other instantaneously with the force of gravity according to his famous inverse square law. Einstein's theory is radically different and mind-bendingly hard to picture. Matter, space, and time are now intimately linked together: the presence of matter causes the fabric of space–time to curve, and the curvature of space–time tells matter how to move.

Newton's theory had bequeathed a significant problem to cosmology, the study of the universe as a whole. If space were an infinite container, as Newton conceived it, containing infinitely many stars, we would be unable to determine the gravitational force on any particular star. On the other hand, if there were only a finite number of stars, the universe would collapse in on itself under gravity. In other words, the universe would be unstable. Einstein set out to solve this problem with his new theory.

To solve his equations of general relativity as applied to the whole universe, and hence begin to answer some of the questions posed in my first paragraph, Einstein and others during the same period made certain simplifying assumptions. One assumption was that the universe is homogeneous, that is to say, the matter of the universe is distributed evenly across space. A second was that the universe is isotropic, meaning that it looks the same in all directions. Of course, these are only approximations. The universe is clearly not totally homogeneous, since it contains galaxies surrounded by near empty space, stars within the galaxies, and so on, and we would not exist if it were totally homogeneous. However, for simplicity, the universe on the largest scale can be treated as a medium of uniform density. It has proved highly profitable up to the present day to make these simplifying assumptions.

Einstein realized that a great advantage of curved space–time is that it allows for the possibility that the three-dimensional universe is finite in size. This is hard to picture, but a two-dimensional analogy can come to our aid (Figure 1.1). Thus the convex surface of a sphere is finite in size, and it is conventional to describe it as having "positive curvature". The surface of a sphere has no boundary or edge and one can travel all the way round it and arrive back at the same place. That would also be possible in a three-dimensional positively curved space, which would bend back on itself in a similar (though hard to picture!) way. A finite universe, Einstein reasoned, might also be stable.

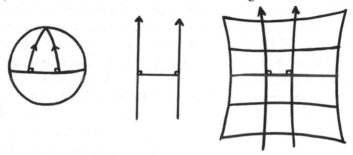

Figure 1.1 In positively curved space, parallel geodesics meet; in our familiar flat Euclidean space, they remain equidistant from each other; and in negatively curved space, they diverge away from each other.

In two dimensions the surface of a sphere has positive curvature, a flat plane has zero curvature, and a saddle shape, which is concave, has negative curvature. We know from our familiar school geometry that the shortest distance between two points is a straight line and that parallel lines in a plane never meet. On curved surfaces, the shortest distance between two points is called a "geodesic". On the surface of a sphere parallel geodesics do meet, and for a saddle shape they diverge away from each other. These surfaces all have their equivalent in three dimensions, though in this case they are much harder to visualize. We have naturally assumed in the past that three-dimensional space is "flat", like the plane in two dimensions, but Einstein is telling us that this naïve picture might be wrong!

Einstein wanted a stable universe and, for philosophical reasons, he also wanted a static universe, a universe that was everlasting, always looking essentially the same. In order to achieve that, in 1917 he introduced an extra term into his equations, which he called the "cosmological constant". This is generally denoted by the Greek letter Λ (capital lambda) and essentially acts like a repulsive force to stretch space. It is thus a kind of anti-gravity force pulling space in the opposite way to gravity. To get a static universe, Einstein had to set this constant Λ arbitrarily to a single unique value, Λ_E (the E subscript denoting the Einstein value), so that gravity and the repulsion were exactly balanced. Einstein was unhappy that the introduction of Λ detracted from the beauty of his theory and later called it a mistake.[2] It turns out that introducing Λ was not a mistake, but setting it to a particular value to obtain a static, eternal universe was.

An important alternative to Einstein's solution was found by the Dutch astronomer Willem de Sitter, also in 1917. This was an empty universe but with a positive cosmological constant. That certainly sounds odd, and Einstein dismissed it as physically unrealistic. Nowadays de Sitter's model is interpreted as an expanding universe solution and a good approximation to the real universe when the matter content has become thinly dispersed due to the expansion.

Enter the Roman Catholic Cleric

In 1927 the Belgian priest Georges Édouard Lemaître came up with a realistic expanding universe solution as an alternative to Einstein's static universe. We now know for sure that the universe is indeed expanding, so this was a vital step in the right direction.

Lemaître had originally trained as an engineer and served in the First World War with distinction, although there is a story of him falling foul of a gunnery instructor when he pointed out an error in the ballistics manual! After the war, Lemaître took up physics, mathematics, and theology. He was ordained priest in 1923 and spent 1923–24 working on his doctoral thesis in Cambridge with the great British astronomer Arthur Eddington, who was famous for verifying general relativity by observing one of the theory's main predictions, the bending of light by the sun. Eddington was a Quaker and a pacifist and risked imprisonment during the First World War. It is fascinating that during the war he wanted to maintain friendship with German scientists, and that immediately after it, in May 1919, he led the solar eclipse expedition that confirmed Einstein's prediction.

I was pleased to discover, not long after arriving at St Edmund's College, Cambridge, myself, that Georges Lemaître had almost certainly resided at the college during the academic year he spent in Cambridge. St Edmund's is only a stone's throw from the University Observatory where Eddington lived and worked. Moreover, in Lemaître's time, St Edmund's House, as it was then known, was a place of residence for Roman Catholic clergy and laity studying and working in the university, with a Roman Catholic chapel where priests could say daily Mass. Now a full college of the university, St Edmund's nevertheless retains, uniquely in Cambridge, a Roman Catholic chapel with a Roman Catholic dean.

The solution to Einstein's equations that Lemaître discovered had in fact already been found in 1922 by the Russian physicist Alexander Friedmann. Indeed Friedmann found a complete set of solutions and gave examples in which the age and mass of the universe were remarkably close to presently accepted values. However, Friedmann had treated all this as simply a mathematical exercise and had never thought to look for observational support. Yet as early as 1912 there was some support for the expanding universe from observations of Doppler shifts in distant nebulae made by Vesto Slipher at the Lowell Observatory in Flagstaff, Arizona.

Doppler shift (Figure 1.2) is the difference between the frequency of light (or sound) received from an object in motion compared to that for the same object at rest. The high-pitched sound of an approaching train becomes lower in pitch when the train is receding. When we observe a distant nebula, we examine the colour spectrum of the light entering our telescopes. This spectrum is crossed by dark lines due to the absorption of light at certain frequencies by the atoms of various chemical elements.

These absorption lines occur as light from the hot interior of stars is absorbed by cooler material in their atmospheres, and the effects from many stars are combined for a nebular spectrum. Slipher observed a preponderance of redshifts (i.e. shifts to lower frequency or, equivalently, higher wavelength) over blueshifts in these absorption lines, indicating that most nebulae were receding from us.

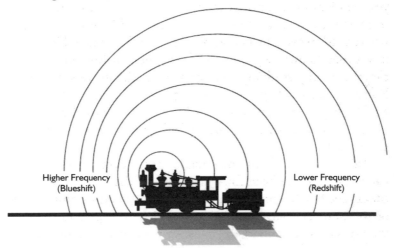

Higher Frequency
(Blueshift)

Lower Frequency
(Redshift)

Figure 1.2 Doppler shift is the change in frequency of sound or light waves received from an object in motion. The frequency is higher for an approaching object and lower for a receding object.

In 1929 Edwin Hubble, working with the 100-inch telescope at Mount Wilson in California, verified the result already found by Lemaître. Hubble measured both the distances and redshifts of distant nebulae, now believed to be galaxies like our own Milky Way galaxy. The redshift determines the velocity, and Hubble showed from this that the velocity of recession of the distant nebulae was directly proportional to their distance. This is known as the Hubble law (Figure 1.3) but was in fact predicted by Lemaître in his 1927 paper. Lemaître had even calculated a value for what is now known as the "Hubble constant", a parameter that measures the rate of expansion, and his value was not very different from Hubble's a couple of years later.

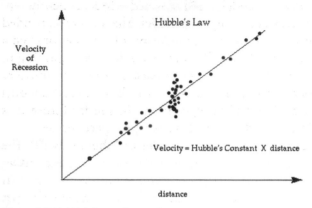

Figure 1.3 Hubble's law: velocity of recession is proportional to distance.

Thus by 1929 Lemaître and Hubble, building on the work of Slipher and others, had shown that, on the largest scale, the galaxies are moving away from each other. In reality, it would be more accurate to say that, according to general relativity, it is the expanding space that is carrying the galaxies with it, rather than the galaxies moving relative to one another. It is like when a balloon is blown up and dots painted on the surface are pulled apart by the expansion of the fabric of the balloon (Figure 1.4).

Figure 1.4 When the balloon is blown up the fabric expands to pull apart the dots (galaxies) painted on it.

The Primeval Atom

We are now on track in the quest for a realistic model of the universe, which we now know to be the Big Bang. However, Lemaître's 1927 model, rediscovered independently of Friedmann, was not yet a Big Bang model. The universe expanded from a finite size, not from a "singularity" of zero size or even a highly compact initial state. There was no definite beginning in this 1927 model, but as one looks back in time the universe approximates more and more closely to an Einstein static model of radius about 900 million light years. In the far future it is more realistic and tends to a de Sitter empty-space model.

Einstein described Lemaître's model as "abominable"![3] The mathematics was fine, but Einstein hated the idea of an expanding universe. However, in 1930 Eddington published a paper in which he recognized that Lemaître had shown Einstein's own model to be unstable.[4] This was particularly devastating since of course one of the motivations for Einstein's model in the first place had been to avoid the instability of Newton's cosmology.

In 1931 Eddington went on to secure the publication of an English translation of Lemaître's 1927 paper in *Monthly Notices of the Royal Astronomical Society*.[5] This would bring Lemaître's work to a much wider audience than could the original paper, which had been published in a relatively obscure Belgian journal. Of course by this time there was increasing evidence in Lemaître's favour from the Hubble expansion.

The year 1931 also saw Lemaître's publication of a new model of the universe, this time with a real temporal beginning.

Figure 1.5 Einstein and Lemaître discussing the origin of the universe at Pasadena, California, in 1933.

It was published as a letter to *Nature* and bore the title "The Beginning of the World from the Point of View of Quantum Theory".[6] He envisaged the initial state of the universe as a single atom with the total mass of the universe, which, being unstable, would divide and divide into smaller atoms by a "kind of super-radioactive process". And, later in the year, at the British Association for the Advancement of Science, Lemaître described how "The whole universe would be produced by the disintegration of this primeval atom."[7]

Lemaître's "primeval atom" provided the first ostensibly physical Big Bang model, comprising the two components of expansion and a beginning in time, and was described in yet another momentous paper of 1931.[8] Whereas Lemaître called it the primeval atom, the term "Big Bang" was coined later by another great British astrophysicist, Fred Hoyle, who hated the idea. Indeed there was a great deal of ideological suspicion of the idea that the universe had a beginning. This suspicion lasted from the time such theories were first mooted until the Big Bang was finally established beyond reasonable doubt by observation of the predicted cosmic background radiation in 1965. This is a story we need to examine in more detail, including the most recent debates, but of course the question lurking in cosmologists' minds was, if the universe had a beginning, did it not therefore require a Creator?

An Unavoidable Singularity?

Interestingly, the new Lemaître model of 1931 retained a cosmological constant, like the model of 1927 (now renamed the Lemaître–Eddington model), whereas Einstein abandoned the cosmological constant in 1931 on the grounds of its ugliness. George Gamow reports Einstein as telling him that he considered the introduction of the cosmological constant Λ his "biggest blunder".[9] That may be apocryphal, but in a letter to Lemaître in 1947 Einstein did write the following, which underlines how important it is to scientists that their theories should be mathematically beautiful:

> Since I have introduced the term I had always a bad conscience. But at the time I could see no other possibility to deal with the fact of the existence of a finite mean density of matter. I found it very ugly indeed that the field law of gravitation should be composed of two logically independent terms which are connected by addition. About the justification of such feelings concerning logical simplicity it is difficult to argue. I cannot help to feel it strongly and I am unable to believe such an ugly thing should be realized in nature.[10]

John Polkinghorne is fond of saying that seeing beauty in mathematics is "an austere form of aesthetic pleasure"! That may resonate with readers who are not mathematically minded, but it is certainly true that mathematical beauty is an important criterion for physicists in evaluating alternative theories.

In 1932 Einstein and de Sitter came up with a further significant solution, which was to them simpler than Lemaître's 1931 model. The Einstein–de Sitter model has zero cosmological constant Λ, but "flat" geometry. Significantly it is also a Big Bang model with a beginning in time from a point of zero size. But it was Lemaître whose pioneering work on the primeval atom led to him being dubbed the "Father of the Big Bang". How pleased he would have been to know that the 2011 Nobel prize for physics was awarded to two teams of astronomers who discovered that the expansion of the universe is accelerating, indicating that the cosmological constant is indeed non-zero as Lemaître continued to maintain. Nowadays, many cosmologists interpret the cosmological constant as something called "dark energy". This is the energy associated with the vacuum in quantum theory, the theory of the very small. Although we tend to think of a vacuum as empty space, in quantum theory it is a sea of activity with particles spontaneously coming into existence and annihilating.

The step Lemaître did not take was to accept Einstein's equations at their face value and conclude that the size of the universe shrinks literally to zero as one takes time back to the origin. For Lemaître the universe began with the primeval atom. The equations on their own, however, indicate that there is what cosmologists refer to as a "singularity" at the beginning – a point at which the density of matter becomes infinite as all the universe's mass is crushed into the singular point. In the 1930s physicists generally thought such a notion was unphysical – and Einstein and Lemaître were among them. Nowadays, thanks largely to the work on "singularity theorems" of Stephen Hawking and Roger Penrose, it is recognized that a singularity is formed by gravitational collapse at the end of the lifetime of some types of star. The resulting object is called a "black hole", and giant black holes are singularities found at the centres of galaxies.

Which Universe Are We in?

As a result of the epochal work of this period, modern cosmologists can classify all the possible models of the universe that result from solving Einstein's equations of general relativity applied to the whole universe under certain simplifying assumptions. These include the assumptions of homogeneity and isotropy we met earlier, namely that the universe looks the same at all places and in all directions. In addition to the persons already mentioned above, two further significant contributors are H. P. Robertson and A. G. Walker. Robertson and Walker worked out the formula for the distance between two points for a homogeneous, isotropic universe. This formula is called the metric and is the generalized form of Pythagoras's theorem for such a four-dimensional space–time. It describes the geometry of space–time, in particular whether space–time is positively or negatively curved or flat. These models of the universe are therefore variously known as Friedmann–Lemaître–Robertson–Walker (FLRW) models, or Friedmann–Robertson–Walker (FRW), or simply Robertson–Walker (RW) models.

Since there is still some doubt as to which precisely of these models most closely applies to the real universe – which, even with the latest observations, lies tantalizingly close to the border between them – it is worth briefly summarizing them at this point. They can be classified according to two parameters, namely the curvature of space–time, which can be negative, positive, or zero (i.e. "flat"), and the cosmological constant Λ, which can also be negative, positive, or zero.

Whether space is curved positively, negatively, or is flat depends on the density of the universe, assumed as noted above to be uniform across space, but in general varying with time. The overall density includes contributions from matter, radiation, and the cosmological constant.

There is a certain critical value of density (varying with time) that gives rise to a flat space–time. If the density is above this value, it will stay above it and space will be positively curved. If below it, space will be negatively curved. For convenience, cosmologists define the parameter Ω (capital omega) to be the mean density divided by the critical value. Then space is flat if Ω is equal to one; space is positively curved if Ω is greater than one; and space is negatively curved if Ω is less than one.

It is important to note that if space is positively curved the universe will be finite in size, like the surface of a sphere in two dimensions: such spaces are called "closed". Models of zero or negative curvature are spatially infinite and in two dimensions resemble a flat plane or a saddle shape respectively: these spaces are called "open".

Effect of the Cosmological Constant

If the cosmological constant Λ is negative, Λ no longer represents a repulsion but an attraction and it reinforces gravity. All the models, of whatever curvature, then begin at a singularity, expand to a maximum size, and recollapse to a "Big Crunch", a final singularity.

If Λ is zero, a positively curved universe will expand from a singularity and then ultimately recollapse. However, in zero and negatively curved universes gravity will not be strong enough to cause recollapse and these universes will expand forever. The flat (zero curvature) model with zero Λ is the Einstein–de Sitter universe and, while this universe does indeed expand forever, the rate of expansion is always decreasing with time. It is just about the simplest model, which is why Einstein favoured it, and for many purposes it is a very good approximation to our own universe. In the Λ zero and negatively curved universe the expansion rate tends to a constant value over time.

If Λ is positive, as now appears to be the case, there are several possibilities. One is the empty de Sitter universe, which simply expands, getting ever faster, forever. Another, when Λ takes the Einstein value Λ_E, is the Einstein static universe of constant radius, eternally existing and unchanging. As described above, the Eddington–Lemaître model (Lemaître's original 1927 model) starts from an Einstein universe and expands forever. The Lemaître "Big Bang" model has Λ greater than the Einstein value. It starts explosively but the expansion rate slows down, then finally it speeds up. This is because gravity dominates to begin with to slow the expansion, but then the cosmological constant takes over and ever more strongly dominates gravity.

The Einstein, Eddington–Lemaître, and Lemaître models all have positive curvature, which means they are finite in size. But there are also models with flat and negatively curved geometry, and matter, which, like the Lemaître model, start from a singularity, slow initially and then accelerate as the cosmological constant dominates. However, the universes described by these models are infinite, whereas the Lemaître model is finite.

Since the present universe is very close to being flat, it remains tantalizingly difficult to ascertain whether it is precisely flat or just curved positively or negatively. Still, we have come a long way, and even by the 1930s it was looking promising that some of the questions posed at the beginning of this chapter were amenable to scientific answers. But then a group of Cambridge cosmologists threw a spanner in the works and challenged the whole Big Bang concept. Maybe we are not in any of the universes I have described.

A Rival on the Block[11]

By the 1940s, the evidence of the redshifts, interpreted as due to the expansion of the universe, seemed to indicate that some version of the Big Bang theory was correct. The Einstein static, eternal universe did not seem to reflect reality. However, a major challenge remained. The age of the universe had been estimated from the Hubble law to be a couple of billion years or even less. However, this was smaller than the estimated age of stars and galaxies, and indeed of the earth itself. It was pretty troubling that cosmological theory gave an age of the universe less than that of some of the objects within it! More accurate observations came much later, from the early 1950s on. Today, observations from the European Space Agency's Planck satellite yield an estimate of the age of about 13.8 billion years, comfortably older than the objects within it, and the three significant figures[12] indicate how far cosmology has advanced as a science of measurement. Incidentally, this figure updates the earlier remarkably accurate estimate of 13.7 billion years obtained by the WMAP (Wilkinson Microwave Anisotropy Probe) satellite.

Possibly even more important than this age problem was the ideological objection to the idea that the universe had a beginning. We have seen that Einstein disliked the idea. Eddington, who, although a Quaker, wanted to keep religion and science apart, was equally critical, writing in 1931 that "philosophically, the notion of a beginning of the present order of Nature is repugnant to me."[13] And Helge Kragh writes that astronomers in general preferred to speak of the "cosmic time scale" rather than to date the present epoch from an absolute beginning of time.[14] Indeed "most astronomers preferred to neglect what may seem to be a natural consequence of the evolutionary, relativistic worldview."[15]

In 1948 the view that there was any kind of evolution at all was challenged by a new theory, which ran directly contrary to the Big Bang idea. As formulated by Thomas Gold and Hermann Bondi in that year, it was based on a metaphysical principle called the "perfect cosmological principle".[16] This principle states that not only does the universe on the largest scale present a uniform aspect at every place within it, but it presents the same uniform aspect at every time in its history. Previous cosmological models had assumed uniformity across space, but to assume uniformity at all times as well was new. Put simply, the universe looks the same at any place and any time, always excluding local irregularities. It should be stressed that this is indeed a metaphysical or philosophical principle, not an empirical scientific principle derived from observation or experiment.

In order to account for the observed expansion it was necessary in the steady-state theory that new matter come into existence in the space created between the receding galaxies, and at just the right rate. In fact, other steady-state continuous creation models had arisen in the pre-war period, quite often associated with a metaphysical preference for God to be continuously creating rather than, as it were, winding up the universe at the beginning and letting it run down. Physicists such as Robert Millikan and many others put forward such highly speculative steady-state type theories, and in 1933 such ideas were endorsed from the theological perspective by W. R. Inge, the well-known Dean of St Paul's Cathedral.[17]

Inge (pronounced, as he said himself, to rhyme with "sting" not "whinge") was something of a maverick. He was an advocate of Christian mysticism and wrote popular and witty columns for several newspapers. He was known as "the gloomy Dean" for his pessimism about the state of modern society. In his book *God and the Astronomers* he hoped that some such scheme as Millikan's would be found whereby some process compensated for the expansion. He was unhappy with the idea of the Creator starting the universe off and saw the divine origin of the universe much more in terms of its orderly and value-laden character.[18]

Despite all this, there seems to have been an atheist agenda behind the steady-state theory proper put forward by Bondi, Gold, and, significantly, Fred Hoyle, who simultaneously came up with a rather different version of the theory. Nevertheless the steady-state theory still attracted Christian support, notably from the cosmologist W. H. McCrea. Moreover, the Anglican theologian E. L. Mascall noted how it was entirely in keeping with Aquinas's notion of God both bringing things into existence and preserving them in existence so that "if he withdrew his action from them, all things would be reduced to nothing."[19]

Kragh tells us that it was particularly Hoyle who objected to a singular creation event which was beyond the realm of scientific understanding.[20] In his 1948 paper Hoyle wrote: "For it is against the spirit of scientific enquiry to regard observable effects as arising from 'causes unknown to science', and this is in principle what creation-in-the-past implies."[21] Another reason the trio rejected standard cosmology was the time-scale problem. This could be solved in the Lemaître and other evolutionary models but at the unacceptable cost of fine-tuning the cosmological constant. This was deemed a fudge which ought to be unnecessary in a true theory, though it is interesting that Hoyle, in a lecture in 1960, acknowledged that Lemaître's model could do the trick.[22]

Interestingly enough, Hoyle initially objected to matter creation, as suggested by Gold, and this delayed progress on the steady-state theory.[23] After all, matter creation would constitute a violation of the law of conservation of energy. In the event, this would mean that two versions of the steady-state theory would emerge, both in 1948, one authored by Hoyle and the other by Bondi and Gold. Another very significant difference within the trio is that, unlike Hoyle, Bondi and Gold regarded general relativity as suspect when extrapolated to apply to the universe as a whole.

In his version of the theory, Hoyle modified Einstein's equations of general relativity by replacing the cosmological term with a "creation tensor", which did, after all, violate the law of energy conservation! The rate of matter creation governed by the creation tensor just matches the rate at which matter disappears across the horizon of the visible universe. But Hoyle preferred his approach to that of Bondi and Gold who started instead from the abstract "perfect cosmological principle". For Hoyle, that principle was a consequence of his theory rather than an unproved assumption you start from like an axiom in mathematics. In contrast, Bondi and Gold judged it necessary to ensure that the laws of physics did not change over time, and they claimed that without such a principle cosmology could not be counted a science.[24]

At this stage I could suggest that perhaps a theological principle would have done what Bondi and Gold wanted! They are right that some metaphysical principle is required to undergird the constancy of physical laws. Theologians would say that this principle is the faithfulness of God. The constancy of physical laws is a sign of God's reliability in maintaining those laws, and the God of the Christian religion is not capricious but faithful. This kind of view informed the natural philosophers of the "scientific revolution", such as Johannes Kepler who reputedly saw himself "thinking God's thoughts after him" when uncovering the laws of planetary motion. No science at all is possible without some sort of presupposition about there being order and law-like behaviour out there to be discovered. Why that should be the case is not explained by science, but it is explained by theology. However, it is not an explanation that would have appealed to the atheistic proponents of the steady-state theory.

The perfect cosmological principle implies that the Hubble expansion rate we observe today is the same as that at all times, past, present, and future. This enabled Bondi and Gold to calculate, very straightforwardly and without any appeal to general relativity, the rate of creation of matter required to balance the expansion. In Bondi's book, which utilized an up-to-date figure for the Hubble constant, he gave an imperceptibly tiny rate of something like the equivalent of one hydrogen atom per litre coming into existence every 500 billion years.[25] Hoyle put it more graphically in his 1950 radio broadcasts as one atom per year in a volume equal to that encompassed by St Paul's Cathedral. Clearly this is many orders of magnitude below any detectable threshold![26]

One of the most bitter disputes in all cosmology was occasioned by Hoyle's defence of the steady-state theory. It involved the future Nobel prize-winning Cambridge radio astronomer Martin Ryle and was mainly concerned with counts of radio sources, once these were established to be extragalactic (which Ryle originally denied but Hoyle rightly asserted), relative to their brightness. If the steady-state theory is correct then sources of a given brightness should be uniformly distributed throughout space. There is then a simple and easily derivable formula for the number of sources having a brightness greater than any particular value.[27] This formula can easily be tested by drawing a simple graph based on actual observations.

From about 1954 onwards Ryle sought to catalogue radio sources and to disprove the steady-state theory. Indeed, he apparently achieved results which did that, obtaining a graph different from that which the steady-state theory predicted. The trouble was that the survey results Ryle presented in 1954 (from the second of a series of Cambridge surveys) were unreliable; they were contradicted by observers in Australia, and the survey results of 1958 (from the third Cambridge survey) were still disputed. However, by 1961 further results were much more accurate, were confirmed by other observers, and did indeed seem to refute the steady-state theory. These latter results were further confirmed by the complete fourth Cambridge survey carried out between 1958 and 1964, though the steady-state advocates stuck to their guns despite the mounting evidence. It was in reality the discovery of the cosmic microwave background radiation in 1965 that provided the clinching evidence in favour of the Big Bang, and we return to that in the next chapter.

2

THE BIG BANG TRIUMPHS

"Your years of toil,"
Said Ryle to Hoyle,
"Are wasted years, believe me.
The steady state
Is out of date.
Unless my eyes deceive me,

My telescope
Has dashed your hope;
Your tenets are refuted.
Let me be terse:
Our universe
Grows daily more diluted!"

Said Hoyle, "You quote
Lemaître, I note,
And Gamow. Well, forget them!
That errant gang
And their Big Bang –
Why aid them and abet them?

You see, my friend,
It has no end
And there was no beginning,
As Bondi, Gold,
And I will hold
Until our hair is thinning!"

From a poem by Barbara Gamow[1]

The Role of Ideology: Fred Hoyle[2]

We have begun to see already that ideological factors were at work when both the Big Bang and steady-state theories were being developed, so let us look at this a little more closely. It was particularly the militant atheist steady-state theorists for whom a beginning of the universe was a problem, and it remains true today that atheist cosmologists are troubled by the idea of a beginning.

Simplicity

One feature common to many of the scientists on both sides of the Big Bang versus steady-state divide is the search for simplicity. Lemaître, influenced by Einstein, wrote in 1922: "Scientific progress is the discovery of a more and more comprehensive simplicity."[3] Einstein himself in 1931 rejected his earlier espousal of a positive cosmological constant because of its ugliness and lack of simplicity. Bondi and Gold appealed to the principle of simplicity to justify giving priority to the perfect cosmological principle over the principle of conservation of matter/energy which, given the non-detectability of new matter, could be regarded as only approximate.

The idea that the simplest of competing hypotheses is most likely to be true has been a useful guiding principle in science. However, one could regard the Bondi–Gold theory as too little driven by observational evidence. This was a point made by physicist and philosopher of science Herbert Dingle in an address he made in 1953 as President of the Royal Astronomical Society. Dingle likened the perfect cosmological principle to abstract ideas of perfection held by Plato and Aristotle which dictated how the world should be, for example in exhibiting "perfectly circular orbits and immutable heavens".[4] Surely conservation of energy and the validity of physical laws across space and time are as simple assumptions to make as is compatible with observation and experiment. Is it not preferable to seek solutions in terms of current well-established physical theories before amending those theories or abandoning them altogether and applying overarching metaphysical principles? Eddington was another scientist who, in his search for a "fundamental theory", which occupied most of his life from the 1930s, was adopting a more Platonic approach.

On the other hand, I think Hoyle would be in the majority among scientists in downplaying grand metaphysical principles, and he hardly discussed the philosophy of science. However, he did not simply embrace the alternative empiricist approach – that based purely on observational or experimental evidence – either. Rather, rightly I think, he noted that no empirical facts, that is, results of observation or experiment, are bare or uninterpreted facts. We always bring some prior theoretical framework to the observations or experiments we make. Thus, for Hoyle, theory and observation go hand in hand.[5] While Bondi shared this view, as Kragh notes, he was more emphatic and provocative in claiming that errors in observation are likely to be more frequent than errors in theory.[6] While observation was of course still deemed important, these views gave the steady-state cosmologists grounds for resisting apparently falsifying data, as well as for having postulated a completely undetectable rate of creation of new matter.

Religion

It is in the area of religion where there is the greatest ideological divide. There are two major questions where modern cosmology and theology potentially interact. The first relates to whether the universe had a temporal origin or not. This is not really a problem for theology, as is evidenced by the support for the steady-state theory of theologians such as Mascall who see it as entirely compatible with the theology of St Thomas Aquinas. Nevertheless, it is the case that a temporal origin is perceived to be a problem by atheists, up to and including Stephen Hawking in the present day. If we can get rid of the temporal origin it is claimed, falsely of course, that we then get rid of God. The second question relates to the special way in which the Big Bang and the laws of physics need to be set up in order for the universe to give rise to life – the so-called fine-tuning – and we return to this shortly. Both these areas of interaction are explored in more detail in subsequent chapters.

We have seen that Hoyle disliked the notion of an initial cause beyond the realms of science, which is what seems to be implied by the Big Bang, and he certainly associated the steady-state theory with atheism.[7] Indeed he freely expressed an emotional preference for the steady state even though he saw that this in itself was irrelevant to its acceptance.[8]

In the last chapter of his book *The Nature of the Universe* – "Man's Place in the Expanding Universe" – he explains why he believes the steady-state theory to be superior to the Big Bang. There are physical reasons such as the time-scale problem and difficulties to do with galaxy formation, and with either theory one is faced with the problem of creation. However, Hoyle is clear about his preference:

> In the older theories all the material in the Universe is supposed to have appeared at one instant of time, the whole creation process taking the form of one big bang. For myself I find this idea very much queerer than continuous creation.[9]

Incidentally, this book transcribes Hoyle's further radio broadcasts of 1950 and we have in it the reoccurrence of the term "big bang", which, however, may not necessarily be pejorative.[10]

At the end of this chapter Hoyle adds a personal reflection, in which he writes this about religion:

> … it seems to me that religion is but a blind attempt to find an escape from the truly dreadful situation in which we find ourselves. Here we are in this wholly fantastic Universe with scarcely a clue as to whether

our existence has any real significance. No wonder
then that many people feel the need for some belief
that gives them a sense of security, and no wonder that
they become very angry with people like me who say
that this security is illusory.[11]

It is no surprise that Hoyle's broadcasts gave rise to considerable
controversy, and indeed the long-running dispute with Ryle
began at about the same time.[12] A number of scientists criticized
Hoyle for his too unqualified presentation of his own speculative
theory. In July 1950 Herbert Dingle was allowed to say as much
in a responding broadcast. The novelist Dorothy L. Sayers was
also allowed to do something similar with respect to Hoyle's
views on religion, which had occasioned the ire of Geoffrey
Fisher, Archbishop of Canterbury, among others. Simon Mitton
tells how Fisher used his speech on receiving an honorary degree
from Manchester University to lambast Hoyle. It happened
that the Chairman of Governors of the BBC, Lord Simon of
Wythenshawe, was there to hear this. Lord Simon turned
to Sydney Goldstein, Professor of Applied Mathematics at
Manchester, for expert advice. Goldstein said of Hoyle's lectures:
"If they want entertainment, the lectures are fine. If they want
science they are not fine. The best astronomers would not agree
with many of his conclusions. Hoyle has not the humility of a
good scientist."[13]

A critical response to Hoyle's views on religion in *The
Nature of the Universe* came from the Australian Broadcasting
Commission, who recruited Daniel O'Connell to speak.
O'Connell was an Irish astronomer, Director of the Vatican
Observatory, and adviser on science to the Pope. He said this:
"The fact is that, though Hoyle sets out expressly to teach
philosophers and theologians their business, he makes no
serious attempt to find out what they hold, or what reasons they
give for their beliefs."[14] A complaint which could equally well be
applied to some of today's scientistic atheists!

I think it is fair to say that Hoyle was a great scientist, despite his lack of humility. He was a bluff Yorkshireman who advanced controversial theories and engaged in polemical disputes throughout his life, as we have seen with Ryle. One of Hoyle's aphorisms was "it is better to be interesting and wrong than boring and right."[15] And this is something the great man lived up to!

Further association of the steady-state theory with atheism occurs in Hoyle's book *Frontiers of Astronomy*. The theory contrasts with the Big Bang, which requires the acceptance of starting conditions "which we are obliged to accept as conditions arbitrarily imposed for no reasons that we understand". He writes:

> This procedure is quite characteristic of the outlook of primitive peoples, who in attempting to explain the local behaviour of the physical world are obliged in their ignorance of the laws of physics to have recourse to arbitrary starting conditions. These are given credence by postulating the existence of gods, gods of the sea... gods of the mountains, gods of the forests... and so forth.[16]

It seems to me, in contrast to Hoyle, that physics normally proceeds precisely by applying the laws to a set of starting conditions to see how a system evolves. It is in cosmology now, as in Hoyle's day, where the avoidance of starting conditions is uniquely being sought.

Elsewhere Hoyle expresses what he sees as the gulf between the way science and religion work. In a lecture given in 1957 at Great St Mary's, the University Church, in Cambridge he said this:

> Religious thought is not controlled by the requirement that it must make correct predictions concerning

the events that take place in the external world. It is controlled by doctrines usually laid down many centuries ago in canonical forms, in the Bible for the Christian, in the Koran for the Muslim. The existence of these written doctrines would seem to make any rooted change of outlook difficult to achieve.[17]

In a similar vein Roman Catholicism, like Communism, argues by dogma:

An argument is judged "right" by these people because they judge it to be based on "right" premises, not because it leads to results that accord with the facts. Indeed if the facts of the case should disagree with the dogma then so much worse for the facts.[18]

Hoyle shares with the religious person a sense of awe before the universe and the sense that there must be some "deep laid purpose" there. It is the particularities of religion that he rejects, such as miracles (which he sees as God constantly correcting his own poor handiwork when things go wrong)[19] and, in the case of Christianity, such specific doctrines as the divinity of Christ and the Virgin Birth. Indeed Hoyle is utterly scathing about such beliefs, which amount to a "denial of rational thought" and "contradict the very fabric of the world."[20] Hence they "negate the faculty which separates Man from the beasts." He states: "Religion, if it is not to be pernicious nonsense, must be based on rational thinking."[21] If religion *were* to change its dogmas, in the way science does, such changes would have to be on the scale of seeing Jesus as just an exceptional man rather than God incarnate.[22]

Hoyle's view of religion is naïve in a number of ways. Religion may not be predictive – and there are other areas of human enquiry that are not predictive, such as ethics and history – but it *is* explanatory. Scientific laws codify the regularities normally observed in nature. They have nothing to say about singular instances, which miracles are. And Christian doctrines can be regarded as rationally formulated responses to historical evidence and the experience of the Church.

As an example of the explanatory role of religion, the doctrine of the *imago dei* – that human beings are made in the image of God – explains why the inherent logic of the human brain parallels the structure of the universe as a whole. Hoyle recognizes and alludes to this fact but circumvents it by identifying God with the universe.[23] Quite how the universe manages to create a pattern of itself inside our heads, as Hoyle believes it does, remains unclear, but for him: "The Universe constitutes everything that there is."[24]

The first chapter of Hoyle's 1977 book *Ten Faces of the Universe*[25] is called "God's Universe" and in it Hoyle launches another tirade against Christian belief. He remarks that "the attributes of God so frequently and confidently announced from the pulpit were quite indefensible" and lists some of them: "God the father – i.e. the family man; God the maker of all things – i.e. a craftsman or artisan; God almighty – a war leader; God in heaven, wherever that may be."[26] Rather than engaging with what theologians say about these matters, Hoyle contents himself with remarking that they are "plainly man-made" and "without meaning".[27] Again, only equating God with the universe makes any sense to him. His solution to the Northern Ireland problem would have been to "arrest every priest and clergyman in Ireland and to commit every man jack of them to long jail sentences on the charge of causing civil war."[28] After all, the violence is simply due to priests and clergymen instilling "nonsense words and concepts" into children, and different nonsense words at that into Roman Catholic and Protestant children.

Despite this negativity towards religion, Hoyle does, however, recognize as significant the second area in which cosmology and religion interact, namely that concerning the "fine-tuning". Thus he notes that there are very surprising connections between the origin of life, the building up of chemical elements in stars, and the laws of nuclear physics. These connections are either "random quirks"[29] or signs of a super-intellect behind the universe.[30]

Hoyle made a famous prediction to do with the way carbon, the key element necessary for life, is manufactured in stars through nuclear reactions. It is made by crashing three helium nuclei together. Since helium nuclei are also known as alpha particles this is known as the "triple-alpha" reaction (Figure 2.1). The problem is that the intermediate element beryllium, with two helium nuclei combined, is unstable and lasts for only a fleeting fraction of a second. Hoyle realized that there had to be an effect that makes the production of carbon proceed efficiently. He predicted something called a "resonance" in the carbon nucleus which would do the trick. A resonance is a very precise value of the energy the carbon nucleus can take which ensures that beryllium captures a further helium nucleus, to make carbon, before it decays.

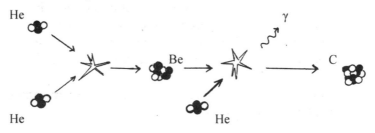

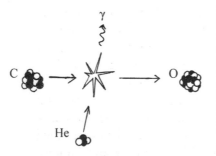

Figure 2.1 The element beryllium is formed by the fusion of two helium nuclei, each comprising two protons and two neutrons. Carbon is formed by the fusion of another helium nucleus with beryllium, and gamma (γ) radiation is emitted. Then oxygen is formed by the fusion of yet another helium nucleus with carbon, again with the emission of gamma radiation. The text explains how these reactions are "fine-tuned" to produce the right amounts of carbon and oxygen for life to be possible in the universe.

This is only part of the story. At the same time, it turned out that there was an energy level in oxygen just below that which would make the production of oxygen resonant; that is, efficient in a similar way. Oxygen is made from crashing a further helium nucleus into a carbon nucleus. If that reaction were resonant, *all* the carbon would be turned into oxygen. Hoyle realized, of course, that both carbon and oxygen are required for the universe to give rise to life, and this is the only way these elements can be made.

It is worth quoting Hoyle more extensively on this point. In the Great St Mary's lecture he said this:

> If this were a purely scientific question and not one that touched on the religious problem, I do not believe that any scientist who examined the evidence would fail to draw the inference that the laws of nuclear physics have been deliberately designed with regard to the consequences they produce inside the stars. If this is so, then my apparently random quirks have become part of a deep laid scheme. If not, then we are back again to a monstrous sequence of accidents.[31]

In an article of 1981 he referred to the energy levels in carbon and oxygen being just right for life in these terms:

> If you wanted to produce carbon and oxygen in roughly equal quantities by stellar nucleosynthesis, these are just the two levels you would have to fix, and your fixing would have to be just about where these levels are actually found to be. Is that another put-up, artificial job? Following the above argument, I am inclined to think so. A commonsense interpretation of the facts suggests that a superintellect has monkeyed with physics, as well as with chemistry and biology, and that there are no blind forces worth speaking

about in nature. The numbers one calculates from the facts seem to me so overwhelming as to put this conclusion almost beyond question.[32]

To me it seems difficult to reconcile these remarks with the minimalist religious view expressed by Hoyle earlier whereby God is identified with the universe. Persons are intelligent, not the universe, and the Christian God is conceived as personal. Hoyle's alternative to this, in *The Intelligent Universe*, is a considerable degree of speculation to do with backwards and forwards causation in time:

(i) Information comes from the future to control quantum events in a manner similar to that which the physicist John Wheeler has argued for. In quantum theory, the theory of the very small, a system is not in a definite state until a measurement is made. Bizarre as it may sound, a particle may be in any number of places at the same time, and only end up in one particular place when its position is measured. Wheeler, who incidentally coined the term "black hole", believed that we human beings bring about reality by making measurements, and the reality of the past into the bargain. It is pretty weird but, according to Wheeler, we create the past history of the universe by our measurements, and of course, by analogy, what goes for us and the past goes for some future intelligence and us!

(ii) Life-bearing information is transferred into new forms from past to future along lines popularized more recently by Frank Tipler and resulting in "collective immortality". Tipler sees intelligent life as simply computing or information processing and, he says, it will ultimately take over the whole universe, and infinitely many computations will be performed in the dying fraction of a second of a collapsing universe – a rather strange view of "immortality"!

(iii) These two time flows of information are interrelated thus for Hoyle: "We are the intelligence that preceded us in its new material representation – or rather, we are the re-emergence of that intelligence, the latest embodiment of its struggle for survival."[33]

This highly paradoxical-sounding scheme appears to resemble the closed quantum causal loops invoked by Wheeler and more recently Paul Davies. These authors recognize the obvious fact that we are caused by past events, but they also see us as causing the past! I was kindly invited by Paul Davies, a cosmologist I admire enormously, to debate with him and others when he launched his book *The Goldilocks Enigma* at Imperial College in 2006. I remember a physicist colleague of Davies calling the idea of closed causal loops in quantum theory "mumbo-jumbo", so the reader can be forgiven for struggling with the idea! Hoyle, however, recognizes the similarity of the quantum controller in (i) both to the Christian God outside the universe and to Greek deities who manage an existing cosmos. The advantage of his scheme, as he sees it, is that God's existence is also dependent on the universe – the exact reverse of the Christian view.

Hoyle also sees attacks on the steady-state theory in the 1950s as arising "because we were touching on issues that threatened the theological culture on which western civilization was founded" whereas the "big bang theory requires a recent origin of the Universe that openly invites the concept of creation".[34]

The Role of Ideology: Georges Lemaître

Clearly Lemaître was in the opposite camp to Bondi, Gold, and Hoyle in the matter of religion. But how did it affect his approach to cosmology? (Bondi incidentally later became President of the British Humanist Association and of the Rationalist Press Association – a really serious atheist!)

Odon Godart and Michal Heller discovered an unpublished manuscript from about 1922 in which Lemaître states that the universe began with light just as Genesis had suggested. However, Godart further notes that "Lemaître was too careful a scientist to build his theory on what was no more than an intuitive opinion; a scientific basis was necessary."[35]

According to Kragh, Lemaître's theology may have influenced his preference for a spatially finite universe (positive curvature) over an infinite universe. The finitude of the universe was asserted by Aquinas and goes back to Aristotle, though at times an infinite universe had also been postulated, for example by Cardinal Nicholas of Cusa in the fifteenth century. This is interesting, since it is again a matter which is in dispute in recent philosophical discussion of cosmology. Indeed some, including George Ellis and the philosopher William Lane Craig, have questioned whether an infinite number of physical things, as opposed to infinities treated in pure mathematics, can actually exist. In any case an infinity can always be added to and is never "complete".

Again according to Kragh, Lemaître could not take the steady-state theory seriously, mainly because it differed so radically from his own view, but possibly also because he thought it incompatible with his theology.[36] However, none of this implies that he had advanced his own theory from theological motives, and indeed the weight of evidence is that he did not consider his theory to have any intrinsic theological significance. In this regard, the following quotation is particularly apposite:

As far as I can see, such a theory [of the primeval atom] remains entirely outside any metaphysical or religious question. It leaves the materialist free to deny any transcendental Being. He may keep, for the bottom of space-time, the same attitude of mind he has been able to adopt for events occurring in non-singular places in space-time.[37]

In 1952 there arose a notable disagreement between Lemaître and Pope Pius XII when the latter ventured to suggest that the Big Bang theory supported the doctrine of creation.[38] The Pope had addressed the Pontifical Academy of Sciences on 22 November 1951 in the following terms, where I have added translations of the Latin:

Clearly and critically, as when it [the enlightened mind] examines facts and passes judgment on them, it perceives the work of creative omnipotence and recognizes that its power, set in motion by the mighty *Fiat* of the Creating Spirit billions of years ago, called into existence with a gesture of generous love and spread over the universe matter bursting with energy. Indeed, it would seem that present-day science, with one sweep back across the centuries, has succeeded in bearing witness to the august instant of the primordial *Fiat Lux* ["Let there be light"], when, along with matter, there burst forth from nothing a sea of light and radiation, and the elements split and churned and formed into millions of galaxies...

What, then, is the importance of modern science in the argument for the existence of God based on change in the universe? By means of exact and detailed research into the large-scale and small-scale worlds it has considerably broadened and deepened the empirical foundation on which the argument rests, and from which it concludes to the existence of an *Ens a se* [completely self-sufficient Being], immutable by His very nature... Thus, with that concreteness which is characteristic of physical proofs, it has confirmed the contingency of the universe and also the well-founded deduction as to the epoch when the world came forth from the hands of the Creator. Hence, creation took place. We say: therefore, there is a Creator. Therefore, God exists![39]

Lemaître, usually irrepressibly cheerful, was deeply unhappy about this. Scientifically it portrayed science as unequivocal about the Big Bang, which was certainly not the case. The Big Bang was still a hypothesis and had a strong rival in the steady-state theory. Ernan McMullin recalls Lemaître saying that the universe could easily have gone through a previous phase of contraction.[40] Indeed George Gamow, who, as I shall describe in the next section, did so much important work on the Big Bang in the late 1940s, thought the same, as related in his book *The Creation of the Universe*.[41] In addition, Lemaître thought it confirmed the suspicions of Hoyle and others of a theological agenda behind the Big Bang. Lemaître had himself steered clear of such arguments. Thus he commented neither on Hoyle's atheistic assertions in his BBC broadcasts, which resulted in *The Nature of the Universe*, nor on the opposite argument from the Big Bang to God advanced in the 1940s by the great mathematician, and Roman Catholic convert, E. T. Whittaker, whom, incidentally, the Pope quoted in his controversial address.[42]

Theologically the Pope's statement confused creation, which is inaccessible to science, with origination, which is what science could investigate – essentially the same mistake as Hoyle! Lemaître intervened with the Pope's science adviser, Daniel O'Connell, and succeeded in dissuading the Pope from further ventures into scientific territory, which Lemaître deemed unhelpful.

To Lemaître, theology and science were two different realms, two different paths to truth. Indeed, as he once said: "There were two ways of arriving at the truth. I decided to follow them both."[43] Having been a scientist and now an ordained priest in the Church of England, I rather warm to that!

Lemaître was, naturally, very far from being a fundamentalist. To believe that the Bible teaches science is like "assuming that there must be authentic religious dogma in the binomial theorem". If the Bible is right about immortality and salvation, it is simply fallacious to believe it is right about everything else – that is completely to miss the point of why we were given the Bible in the first place.[44]

When quantum theory pioneer Paul Dirac said to Lemaître that he thought cosmology was the branch of science closest to religion, Lemaître disagreed, saying he thought psychology was the closest.[45]

Lemaître differed from Hoyle fundamentally about cosmology and, even more so, religion – and we have noted Hoyle's view of priests! All the evidence, however, would indicate that these two great scientists got on very well at the personal level. John Farrell tells us about a two-week drive Hoyle, his wife Barbara, and Lemaître took together through Italy and the Alps in 1957. They were dining one night, which happened to be a Friday. Hoyle ordered a steak and Lemaître fish. When the food came, Hoyle's steak was of moderate size, whereas Lemaître's fish was enormous. Hoyle commented, "Now at last, Georges, I see why you are a Catholic!" at which Lemaître became "red-faced and peevish". Hoyle was puzzled, thinking he had committed some terrible "religio-diplomatic indiscretion" as he put it. That was until he remembered that Lemaître hated fish![46]

The theological points in this section will be explored more fully in subsequent chapters. Meanwhile we need to turn to the vital work of Gamow and his colleagues, which sets the scene for the triumph of the Big Bang in the 1960s.

George Gamow and the Hot Big Bang

At about the same time that Bondi, Gold, and Hoyle were proposing their variants of the steady-state theory, George Gamow and his team were working out the observational consequences of the Big Bang theory. They came up with two major predictions, which were subsequently confirmed by observation. Thus they secured the defeat of the steady-state theory, which could not account for the observational data, and marked out the Big Bang as the theory which is now universally believed by cosmologists to describe the origin and evolution of the universe.

Gamow was born in Odessa in the Ukraine in 1904 and as a schoolboy questioned the Christian dogmas of his upbringing. In particular, he tried an experiment to test the doctrine of transubstantiation, according to which the elements of bread and wine turn into the body and blood of Christ at the Eucharist. Finding that the consecrated bread still looked like bread under a microscope, he remarked, "I think this was the experiment which made me a scientist."

It is a pity if this experiment turned him against religion. Orthodox theology on this point is similar to Catholic theology, according to which no change *should* be detected. St Thomas Aquinas, for example, taught that the "substance" (what the elements actually are) of the transubstantiated elements changes but not the "accidents" (their appearance, chemical composition, etc.) However, the Eastern Orthodox Church has generally been less explicit concerning the mechanism of transubstantiation than the Western Church.

Formation of the chemical elements

In 1948 Ralph Alpher, the son of émigré Russian Jews, was completing his PhD at Johns Hopkins University where he collaborated with Gamow. Alpher had lost his Jewish faith as a teenager and doubted God's existence. Like Gamow he did not think that the Big Bang theory implied any divine action.[47]

In 1948 Gamow and Alpher published a famous paper entitled "The Origin of the Chemical Elements". Gamow, who had a sense of humour, mischievously included another colleague, Hans Bethe, as co-author of the paper, which has therefore gone down in history as the "αβγ" (alpha, beta, gamma – the first three letters of the Greek alphabet) paper. Gamow even tried to persuade another significant collaborator, Robert Herman, to change his name to Delter so that the theory could be dubbed the "αβγδ" (alpha, beta, gamma, delta) theory.[48] As an amusing footnote to the nomenclature, Kragh reports Gamow as saying in 1960: "There was… a rumour that later, when the αβγ theory went temporarily on the rock, Dr. Bethe seriously considered changing his name to Zacharias."[49]

Atomic nuclei consist of a mix of positively charged particles called protons and particles of zero charge called neutrons, with the exception of the hydrogen nucleus, which is simply a single proton. The periodic table of the chemical elements is arranged according to atomic number, which is just the number of protons in the nucleus. Isotopes of any particular element contain the same number of protons but vary in the number of neutrons. The atomic weight of the nucleus is the number of neutrons and protons combined. According to the αβγ theory, the very early universe was hot and dense, and matter was composed of neutrons only. The theory is highly significant for proposing a mechanism for the build-up of the higher elements in the periodic table in the first few minutes of the universe's existence. This happens via the following sequence of events. First, neutrons undergo radioactive decay into protons. The protons then combine with neutrons to form deuterons, which are nuclei of the isotope of hydrogen called deuterium. Deuterons in turn combine to form helium, which has atomic number 2. In the αβγ theory the whole sequence of the periodic table is then supposed to be built up by successive addition and decay of neutrons. While this is not correct, it was a highly significant pointer on the way to the correct theory, which was derived over the next few years.

In fact, at early times, the density of radiation in the universe would have dominated that of matter, a fact which was ignored in the αβγ paper but which substantially alters the picture. Alpher and Herman made a remarkable prediction as a result of considering the radiation. As time passes, the density of radiation decreases faster than that of matter. There is a crossover point at which the densities are equal. Alpher and Herman assumed that galaxies then start to form, and the legacy today from that period is a background temperature for the universe of about 5 K, i.e. 5 degrees above absolute zero or −268 °C.[50] This they interpreted as "the background temperature which would result from the universal expansion alone".[51] This astonishingly low temperature, which has resulted simply from the expansion and cooling of the universe, is remarkable given that the temperature was in the billions of degrees at the time of element formation and still of the order of thousands of degrees at the crossover point! This was the first major prediction from the Big Bang theory other than the expansion itself and was vitally significant for its final acceptance.

A major correction to this theory was introduced by the Japanese physicist Chushiro Hayashi. Hayashi realized that radiation at the kinds of temperatures pertaining in the first seconds of the universe's existence, namely tens of billions of degrees, would alter the matter content at the time the chemical elements start to be made. Through processes which need not concern us, it turns out that protons are far more numerous than neutrons at this time. That substantially changes what happens next. In particular, since the helium nucleus consists of two neutrons and two protons, and hydrogen consists of just one proton, the ratio of hydrogen to helium left over from the Big Bang can be calculated. Early results showed that helium should constitute between 29 per cent and 36 per cent by weight of the total hydrogen plus helium content.[52] This is somewhat in excess of the observed abundance of about 27 per cent and the problem lay dormant until more refined calculations by Jim Peebles (1966),[53] and by Robert Wagoner, William Fowler, and Fred Hoyle (1967).[54] It is particularly interesting to see Hoyle's role here in confirming the second major prediction of the Big Bang theory, which he disliked so much!

In fact, the universe now overwhelmingly consists of hydrogen and helium with just traces of the other elements, though another problem encountered by the Big Bang theorists was the inability to produce elements heavier than helium. This was because there were no stable elements of atomic weights 5 and 8 and hence, without these intermediate products, there was a "mass gap" that could not easily be bridged in building up the periodic table. In 1954 Gamow conceded that, while not contradicting the Big Bang theory, this was a severe stumbling block and that the answer to heavy element production might be sought instead in nuclear reactions inside stars. Physicists have since discovered reactions that bridge the gap, but it is still the case that only the lightest elements – deuterium, helium, and a small amount of lithium – could be produced in the Big Bang.

An alternative theory and a satisfying synthesis

There was a rival theory of element production inside stars being developed in parallel with Gamow's Big Bang theory. The point is that, like the early universe, the interiors of stars are also hot enough for nuclear reactions to take place. When temperatures reach hundreds of millions of degrees and more, atomic nuclei will collide at high enough speeds to overcome the repulsion due to their electric charges. Indeed, work had been going on under William Fowler on stellar nuclear reactions at the Kellogg Laboratory at Caltech since 1946.

While staying with Fowler at Caltech, Edwin Salpeter – like Bondi and Gold an émigré of Jewish extraction from Vienna – came up with a means of overcoming the mass gap. He proposed the "triple-alpha" process whereby three helium nuclei combine to form a carbon nucleus, with beryllium the unstable intermediate element. This was precisely the reaction, which two years later in 1953, while also staying at Caltech, Hoyle predicted to require a resonance in the carbon atom so that carbon would be produced in sufficient quantity.

The resonance was confirmed experimentally within a couple of weeks and before Hoyle could publish his paper. The further important point is that the conditions for the triple-alpha mechanism to occur existed in the late phase of a red giant star but not in the Big Bang.

Work on stellar nucleosynthesis culminated in the publication in 1957 of a landmark paper by Hoyle, Fowler, and Margaret and Geoffrey Burbidge. This famous paper, universally known by astrophysicists as B^{2}FH, showed how virtually the whole periodic table, the elements from carbon to uranium, could be built up inside stars.[55] These calculations constitute a quite remarkable achievement for modern physics, though the astrophysics community was shocked that the Nobel prize, which this work truly merited, was awarded to Fowler alone in 1983. This is not to denigrate Fowler, who acknowledged Hoyle as the second great influence in his life after his own doctoral supervisor Charlie Lauritsen. Indeed Fowler wrote to Hoyle two weeks after hearing about the award "with a heavy heart" and expressing incomprehension that the prize was not shared between them. I was fascinated to see this letter displayed in St John's College Library during the Cambridge Science Festival of 2011.[56] The reason Hoyle was overlooked may be because he had criticized the 1974 award to Ryle and Antony Hewish for the discovery of pulsars, but excluding their PhD student Jocelyn Bell. Alternatively, it could be because by now Hoyle was pursuing research on "panspermia", the idea that life on earth was seeded from space, generally regarded as rather outlandish by the scientific community.

Despite this triumph, it turned out to be quite impossible that helium could be produced in anything like its observed abundance of about 27 per cent by mass, in stars. As we have seen, Hoyle and colleagues showed (as did Peebles) that just the right amount of helium could be produced in the Big Bang. The irony here of course is that this effectively put a nail in the coffin of Hoyle's own favoured steady-state theory.

What is more, one atom of hydrogen in every 100,000 in the universe today occurs in the form of the heavy isotope deuterium. But deuterium gets destroyed in stellar interiors rather than produced! Again, however, the abundance of deuterium can be accurately calculated as resulting from nucleosynthesis in the Big Bang. Indeed the paper by Wagoner, Fowler, and Hoyle gave good agreement with observations for the deuterium abundance as well as that for helium. A few other light elements that occur in trace amounts, such as lithium, are also explained as originating in the Big Bang.

In the 1950s the Big Bang and stellar interiors were seen as competing sites for the production of the elements heavier than hydrogen. However, we are now in a position to see that it is not a question of either/or. In a nutshell, light element production in the Big Bang and heavy element production in stars combine to give a satisfying and complete account of how the whole periodic table is built up.[57]

The Cosmic Microwave Background Radiation

As we have seen, as far back as 1948 Alpher and Herman predicted the existence of a background radiation at a temperature of about 5 K, stemming from the expansion of the universe. The most important feature of this predicted radiation is that it is in thermal equilibrium at a uniform temperature and bathes the whole universe. This equilibrium would have been achieved in the early universe when the temperature was high enough for the matter to be ionized; that is, for it to consist of simple atomic nuclei such as I have described, and free electrons not bound to nuclei as they are in matter at normal temperatures. In these circumstances the radiation, which can be regarded as bullet-like particles called photons, would have interacted with the matter, particularly by bouncing off the free electrons. Many such interactions lead to thermal equilibrium in which energy is constantly exchanged between the radiation and the electrons so that eventually the number of particles in any particular energy range stays constant. Thermal radiation has a very characteristic spectrum or distribution of wavelengths.

As the universe expands, it cools and the matter recombines, and interactions between matter and radiation cease. The legacy from this early epoch, however, remains, namely the characteristic thermal spectrum of the radiation.

In 1963 Arno Penzias and Robert Wilson (Figure 2.2), of Bell Telephone Laboratories, working at the time at Holmdel near Princeton, detected an unwanted and unexpectedly large noise in their antenna. At first they thought this was due to pigeon droppings in the antenna! Having got rid of the pigeons, they found that the noise was still there. It comprised microwave radiation at an effective temperature of about 3.5 K. Significantly, Penzias and Wilson failed to understand the cosmological implications of this discovery. That came two years later when Robert Dicke and colleagues (notably Jim Peebles) learned of the discovery, though the Nobel prize for it was awarded to Penzias and Wilson in 1978.

Figure 2.2 Arno Penzias (right) and Robert Wilson (left) pictured near the antenna with which they detected the cosmic microwave background radiation, the clinching evidence for the Big Bang theory.

Dicke had previously suggested to Peebles that he calculate the temperature of the relic radiation from the Big Bang. Peebles got a value of about 10 K and sent off a paper to *Physical Review*. The paper was rejected on the grounds that it was repeating work done by Gamow, Alpher, and Herman in the late 1940s![58]

When in 1965 they heard of Penzias and Wilson's discovery, Dicke and Peebles got together with the Bell Labs physicists and published separate papers, comprising observation and theory, in the July 1965 issue of *Astrophysical Journal*.[59] However, only two years later did the Princeton physicists acknowledge the work of Gamow, Alpher, and Herman, with Dicke writing apologetically to Gamow and wishing them to be friends.[60]

Earliest Observation of the Cosmic Background Radiation

Interestingly enough, the cosmic background radiation had already been observed in 1941 by the Australian astronomer Andrew McKellar who was working at the Dominion Observatory of Canada. What McKellar had actually detected was two absorption lines in the spectrum of a certain interstellar molecule, cyanogen (meaning that light from certain stars has been absorbed at two particular wavelengths, in this case at the violet end of the spectrum).[61] The relative strengths of these absorption lines indicated that the molecules were in equilibrium in a bath of radiation at a temperature of about 2.3 K; that is, just below the temperature predicted by Alpher and Herman, and the temperature later observed by Penzias and Wilson, for the cosmic background radiation. Unfortunately no one drew the correct conclusion at the time, although, oddly enough, Fred Hoyle came close in 1956 when he spent some time with Gamow.[62]

While the evidence from the radio source counts and the helium problem was already showing that the writing was on the wall for the steady-state theory, the observation of the cosmic background radiation was seen as of clinching importance. The Big Bang theory explains it quite naturally, and the steady-state theory cannot explain it except by highly contrived means – and even these contrived explanations have had to be abandoned in the face of measurements from the COBE (Cosmic Background Explorer) satellite, the more recent WMAP (Wilkinson Microwave Anisotropy Probe) satellite, and now the European Space Agency's Planck satellite. The latest observations show that the spectrum of the radiation – that is, how the intensity depends on wavelength – is thermal to very high accuracy at a temperature of about 2.7 K. This has an entirely natural explanation on the basis of the Big Bang as stemming from the era, about 380,000 years after the beginning, when the temperature dropped to about 4,000 K and the matter and energy decoupled as the nuclei and free electrons combined to form atoms and molecules.

While the Big Bang theory is thus very well supported by evidence, we shall see in subsequent chapters that there are many interesting questions still open. But we turn now to consider more carefully the first major area of interaction between science and theology noted above: namely, does a beginning to the universe require God to explain it?

3

THE BIG BANG: DOES A BEGINNING REQUIRE GOD?

THE LORD of all, himself through all diffus'd,
Sustains, and is the life of all that lives.
Nature is but a name for an effect,
Whose cause is God. He feeds the secret fire
By which the mighty process is maintain'd,
Who sleeps not, is not weary; in whose sight
Slow circling ages are as transient days;
Whose work is without labour; whose designs
No flaw deforms, no difficulty thwarts;
And whose beneficence no charge exhausts.

William Cowper (1785)[1]

Stephen Hawking and the Creation of the Universe

We saw in the last chapter that Fred Hoyle disliked the Big Bang theory because he thought that, if the universe had a beginning, it would need a Creator. The steady-state theory was deemed more compatible with his atheism.

Stephen Hawking is a cosmologist who has expressed the same view much more recently and, like Hoyle, has come up with theories that apparently do away with the temporal beginning of the universe. On 2 September 2010 the front page of *The Times* presented us with this startling headline: "Hawking: God did not create Universe". Such was the interest in this sensational claim that over the next few days I was invited to give ten radio interviews, including on BBC Radio 4's *PM Programme* and on the BBC World Service – a truly exhausting experience![2]

The claim is based on what Hawking says in his book, co-authored with Leonard Mlodinow, published the week after the article, and entitled *The Grand Design*.[3] Among the claims Hawking and Mlodinow make are the following:

1. There is no need for God to light the blue touch paper and set the universe going, which for Hawking was his only possible role anyway.

2. Philosophy is dead and has been superseded by science.

3. Something called M-theory (see later, pp. 79–80, and especially pp. 121–23) is the ultimate physical "theory of everything".

4. Because there is gravity or the laws of nature, the universe creates itself out of nothing.

5. A multiverse explains the "fine-tuning" of our universe.

I shall critique all of these statements in due course, in this and subsequent chapters, but let me begin with the statement that philosophy is dead. This occurs on the first page. Yet only a couple of pages later Hawking and Mlodinow say they adopt "model-dependent realism", a philosophical position if ever there was one, and a distinctly odd one at that. One might well ask how the reality of the external world can depend upon the mathematical models we construct of that world. Hawking and Mlodinow define their concept by saying that "it is pointless to ask whether a model is real, only whether it agrees with observations. If there are two models that both agree with observation... then one cannot say that one is more real than another."[4] In contrast, the philosophical position known as "critical realism" would say that there is indeed a real world out there and our scientific theories are gaining an ever tighter grasp on that reality. Our models concern real entities, and we are making progress in our understanding of the structure and behaviour of those entities. That would be the view of such figures as John Polkinghorne and Arthur Peacocke, major contributors to the science–religion dialogue in recent decades. It would probably also be the philosophical view assumed by most scientists, if they gave the matter any thought.

Despite what Hawking and Mlodinow say about philosophy their book is permeated by philosophy and this is only one of their philosophical statements.

Hawking and St Augustine

In their book, Hawking and Mlodinow rightly state that St Augustine believed that time is "a property of the world that God created and that time did not exist before the creation".[5] However, then they say, in line with model-dependent realism: "That is a possible model, which is favoured by those who maintain that the account given in Genesis is literally true", but the Big Bang theory is "more useful", even though "neither model can be said to be more real than the other".[6] This is all deeply confused and confusing, not least because (a) Augustine himself did not take Genesis literally and (b) Augustine's view is entirely compatible with the Big Bang theory! As we saw in Chapter 1, according to the Big Bang theory, space and time came into existence together some 13.8 billion years ago. Hawking and Mlodinow themselves admit that it is not clear that we can take time back beyond the Big Bang because the present laws of physics may break down there. Despite their anti-religious stance, it is good that these authors at least acknowledge the seminal work of Roman Catholic priest Georges Lemaître in the development of the Big Bang model.[7]

I agree with Hawking and Mlodinow that it is very interesting to compare the Big Bang theory with what Christian priests and theologians from the past have said about creation. Thus in about AD 200 Clement of Alexandria argued that time came into being with creatures: "And how could creation take place in time, seeing time was born along with things which exist."[8] This Christian way of interpreting the Scriptures is in line with the Jewish way, as exemplified by Philo of Alexandria (c. 20 BC to c. AD 50). Commenting on Genesis 1:1, Philo wrote:

> ... before the world time had no existence, but was created either simultaneously with it, or after it; for since time is the interval of the motion of the heavens, there could not have been any such thing as motion before there was anything which could be moved...[9]

Hawking and Mlodinow are right about St Augustine and time. He is rather better known than Clement or Philo for saying much the same thing. In the early fifth century he wrote this: "And if the sacred and infallible Scriptures say that in the beginning God created the heavens and the earth... then assuredly the world was made, not in time, but simultaneously with time."[10] Augustine saw God as outside or transcending the space–time realm of the universe he created.

In another place Augustine says this:

> With the motion of creatures, time began to run its course. It is idle to look for time before creation, as if time can be found before time... We should, therefore, say that time began with creation rather than that creation began with time. But both are from God. For from Him and through Him and in Him are all things.[11]

He goes on:

He made that which gave time its beginning, as He made all things together, disposing them in an order based not on intervals of time but on causal connections, and thus the creatures which were made all at once could be shown in their perfection by the sixfold repetition of the "day" of creation.[12]

So we can also see here that he did not take the days literally. Rather, the creation was to unfold thanks to the causal connections, elsewhere called "seed-like principles", which God implanted in the creation at the beginning. All this is of course entirely compatible with the Big Bang! However, one thing I ought to mention is that the main point of the Christian doctrine of creation is not to pinpoint a moment when the universe began, but to say that the universe is totally dependent on God every moment, and that would be true even if the universe had an infinite past. As Augustine puts it, "the universe will pass away in the twinkling of an eye if God withdraws His ruling hand."[13] This is an important point to which I shall return in the next chapter, once we have considered an argument based on the temporal beginning of the universe at the Big Bang.

The *Kalām* Cosmological Argument

An important line of argument that has been made in philosophy has been that the modern discovery that the universe had a beginning, all those 13.8 billion years ago, indicates that it must have been created. On the face of it, it certainly seems to chime in neatly with Augustine's view that God created space and time together. It is just the kind of argument which Pope Pius XII expressed so confidently and which horrified Lemaître.

This argument has been expressed with considerable force and erudition in recent years by the evangelical Christian philosopher William Lane Craig,[14] and, with equal force and vigour, by the Roman Catholic apologist Robert J. Spitzer.[15]

Craig acknowledges that the argument is a form of the cosmological argument that has its roots in medieval Islam. It is known as the *kalām* cosmological argument and goes as follows:

1. Everything that begins to exist has a cause of its existence.

2. The universe began to exist.

3. Therefore, the universe has a cause of its existence.

Presented like that, the argument is a logical proof. If one accepts the premises, 1 and 2, then the conclusion, 3, follows by inexorable logic.

On the face of it, premise 1, that everything that begins to exist has a cause of its existence, seems very reasonable. Craig says it is intuitively obvious. Things do not just appear from nothing. Even quantum effects, particles appearing and disappearing in the quantum vacuum, are not something coming from nothing. We generally think of a vacuum as empty space, containing nothing. But even empty space is not "nothing" in the philosophers' meaning of "nothing", and the vacuum in quantum theory is very far from being "nothing". Indeed the question arises as to how anything could possibly come from absolutely nothing; that is, from the absence of anything at all prior to it.

Premise 2, that the universe began to exist, seems to be precisely what the Big Bang theory is saying. The universe began 13.8 billion years ago. However, I think there are reasons, both scientific and theological, to be cautious about drawing too definite a conclusion about this – or at least, reasons to be cautious in treating it as a deductive proof for God's existence rather than a more modest pointer towards his probable existence. We explore these reasons in the next section.

Did the Universe have a Beginning?

Scientifically, while there are good reasons to believe that the universe had a beginning in time, and I shall give some more in a moment, there are also reasons for caution. A major problem is that, essentially, as one goes back further in time towards the beginning, the physics which applies gets much less secure. In the classical framework of Einstein's general relativity, in which quantum effects are ignored, we can trace back the history of the universe to its origin 13.8 billion years ago as a point of zero size, and of infinite density and temperature; that is, to a "singularity". When that happens in physics, you normally conclude that something is wrong. There are a number of theories on offer which attempt to get round that problem, all of which are highly speculative. The problem scientifically is that we have no single agreed theory that combines quantum theory and general relativity, which is what is required to handle the physics of the very early universe.

One highly speculative theory is due to Stephen Hawking and his colleague James Hartle. According to the Hartle–Hawking theory, as one goes back towards the beginning space–time gets "smoothed out" and time becomes like a space dimension. Time itself is then "imaginary" in the technical mathematical sense of complex numbers. There is no real number which when multiplied by itself gives the value minus one (-1). Mathematicians simply label the square root of -1 with the letter i and then manipulate combinations of i with other numbers in the usual algebraic manner. Multiples of i are called "imaginary numbers" and more general combinations are called "complex numbers". It proves immensely helpful to do this in many contexts.

The upshot of the Hartle–Hawking proposal is that, at the earliest time we can speak of, the usual three dimensions of space and one of time morph into a four-dimensional space that has no boundary or edge. This is what Hawking calls the "no boundary proposal". It was discussed in *A Brief History of Time*, and it reappears in *The Grand Design*.

In fact, Hawking seems to agree with Craig that if the universe had a beginning – if there was a moment when space and time came into existence – then the universe would need God to create it. He thinks his no boundary proposal does away with a beginning and therefore with any need for God. Here is what he says, now quoting from *A Brief History of Time*:

> There would be no singularities at which the laws of science broke down and no edge of space-time at which one would have to appeal to God or some new law to set the boundary conditions for space-time. One could say: "The boundary condition of the universe is that it has no boundary." The universe would be completely self-contained and not affected by anything outside itself. It would neither be created nor destroyed. It would just BE.[16]

And again:

> So long as the universe had a beginning we could suppose that it had a creator. But if the universe is really completely self-contained, having no boundary or edge, it would have neither beginning nor end; it would simply be. What place, then, for a creator?[17]

In *The Grand Design* Hawking and Mlodinow say the same thing: a universe with no beginning in time has no need for God to "light the blue touch paper" to set it going.[18]

There are serious scientific and philosophical problems with Hawking's proposal. Not least is the idea of imaginary time. In *A Brief History of Time* Hawking discussed philosophical options for the meaning of imaginary time and the four-dimensional space that embraced it "prior", in some doubtful sense, to the emergence of real time. Either these were convenient mathematical devices, or perhaps imaginary time was real and real time our own invention.

Another possibility, which now seems to be Hawking's considered position and in accord with his philosophy of "model-dependent realism", is that it is meaningless to ask which is real since they both exist only in our minds and it is only a matter of which is the more useful description. In fact, this is enough to undermine Hawking's atheistic argument: by his own admission either imaginary time is simply a convenient calculating device, or it is meaningless to ask whether it is real in the ontological sense of actually existing. It seems to me, then, that we are perfectly at liberty to reject it as real.

In addition, if time had really become space-like, i.e. simply a fourth spatial dimension, it is very difficult to see how time could "flow" and the universe evolve from the four-dimensional space at all. The universe might just "BE" as Hawking puts it, but how could it ever "BE" anything other than what it "was" in the spatialized time "era"? As when our equations give solutions of infinite density and so on, so when they make time imaginary, the usual approach is to regard this as an indication that something is wrong. Alternatively one could simply say that our equations can be describing physical reality only as long as measurable quantities take real values. Indeed, in his technical papers Hawking himself seems to recognize this very point, and in those the universe does after all have a beginning, even if a singularity is avoided.[19]

Of course, even if we accept Hawking's mathematics, we do not have to accept his philosophy: we can perfectly well accept only real time in the mathematical sense as ontologically real. We can also quite happily accept the universe beginning, not from a singularity, but from the surface where real three-dimensional space and real time intersect the four-dimensional space where time has become imaginary.

Even the atheist philosopher Quentin Smith, who argues for atheism in debate with William Lane Craig, was moved to remark of Hawking's argument: "This is probably the worst atheistic argument in the history of Western thought."[20]

Hawking has failed to show that the universe did not have a beginning. And he is not alone in that. All the other major theories on offer in modern cosmology also fail to do away with the beginning. These include André Linde's chaotic and eternal inflation models and the ekpyrotic model of Neil Turok and Paul Steinhardt. In the inflation models, there is not a single Big Bang but many different "universes" bubbling up out of a background space (chaotic inflation) or sprouting further universes, which branch off from existing ones (eternal inflation). In the ekpyrotic model, our universe arises from the collision of higher-dimensional "brane" universes. (Note that all the models mentioned here will be explained more fully in Chapter 7.) In either case the whole process would nevertheless still ultimately track back to a singularity, a first moment when all of space–time was contracted to an infinitely dense point of zero size. This is because of a powerful theorem of Arvind Borde and Alexander Vilenkin, according to which, under quite general conditions, such a singularity must exist at some finite time in the past. The original 1994 paper of Borde and Vilenkin applied to inflationary models;[21] a further refinement by Borde, Vilenkin, and Alan Guth in 2001, and updated in 2003, included "brane" cosmologies.[22]

Ironically Alexander Vilenkin reaffirmed the results of his theorems at a meeting in Cambridge in early 2012 convened to celebrate Stephen Hawking's seventieth birthday, as reported by Lisa Grossman in *New Scientist*.[23] Sadly, Hawking could not attend because of illness, but in a pre-recorded message he had said this, in line with his earlier statements: "A point of creation would be a place where science broke down. One would have to appeal to religion and the hand of God." But Vilenkin's results show that models with a single Big Bang, cyclic universes with many big bangs and big crunches, eternal inflationary models, and ekpyrotic models all have a beginning at some finite time in the past – at a point where science does indeed "break down".

The argument against the universe having had an infinite number of cycles is a straightforward consequence of the second law of thermodynamics. The universe is going from a state of high order to states of lower order and, after infinite time, should now be in a state of maximum disorder, i.e. uniform and featureless. This is clearly contrary to observation since, apart from any other consideration, it is incompatible with our own existence! Vilenkin is reported as saying, "All the evidence we have says that the universe had a beginning."[24]

Peter Bussey, a Christian physicist who has carefully and dispassionately reviewed the *kalām* argument in the light of Vilenkin's theorems, concurs: "If the summary of the current position by Vilenkin and others is correct, cosmologies with an infinite past history are not easily viable at present, and so the universe 'probably' had a beginning. Therefore the Kalam argument would seem to hold."[25] What the *kalām* argument then demonstrates, says Bussey, is that a non-temporal and non-physical First Cause for the universe is ultimately unavoidable.

Having said all this, there is also a theological objection to Hawking, and indeed to the whole line of argument towards atheism based on the absence of a beginning. And that leads us to further discussion of the Christian doctrine of creation.

4
THE CHRISTIAN DOCTRINE OF CREATION

He sang of God – the mighty source
Of all things – the stupendous force
    On which all strength depends;
From whose right arm, beneath whose eyes,
All period, power, and enterprise
    Commences, reigns, and ends.

Christopher Smart (1722–70), "Song to David"[1]

The Conflict Myth

Some Christians and some scientists immediately jump to the conclusion that the scientific story and the Christian story of creation are in conflict. That is because they think that Christians understand the creation stories of the Bible literally – or ought to understand them literally if they do not! That is deeply mistaken, essentially because it confuses the mechanism of creation with the theology of creation, and it is the latter that is really important.

Augustine, who featured in the last chapter, recognized that one cannot take both Genesis 1 and Genesis 2 literally. This is a matter internal to the text of Scripture and nothing to do with science. Genesis 1:1 – 2:4a and Genesis 2:4bff. give two different creation stories with a different order of creation. And Genesis 1 certainly cannot be taken literally since you have three 24-hour days before the appearance of the sun on Day 4! This point had also been made forcibly by Origen early in the third century: "Now what man of intelligence will believe that the first and the second and the third day, and the evening and the morning existed without the sun and moon and stars?"[2] Augustine added the further point that evening and morning only succeed each other at a particular location; the earth as a whole experiences both simultaneously.

There is a particularly helpful passage in Augustine that is worth quoting in full as an object lesson to the modern-day biblical literalist:

> Usually even a non-Christian knows something about the earth, the heavens, and the other elements of this world, about the motion and orbit of the stars and even their size and relative positions, about the predictable eclipses of the sun and moon, the cycles of the years and the seasons, about the kinds of animals, shrubs, stones, and so forth, and this knowledge he holds to as being certain from reason and experience. Now, it is a disgraceful and dangerous thing for an infidel to hear a Christian, presumably giving the meaning of Holy Scripture, talking nonsense on these topics; and we should take all means to prevent such an embarrassing situation, in which people show up vast ignorance in a Christian and laugh it to scorn. The shame is not so much that an ignorant individual is derided, but that people outside the household of the faith think our sacred writers held such opinions, and, to the great loss of those for whose salvation we toil, the writers of our Scripture are criticized and rejected as unlearned men. If they find a Christian mistaken in a field which they themselves know well and hear him

maintaining his foolish opinions about our books, how are they going to believe those books in matters concerning the resurrection of the dead, the hope of eternal life, and the kingdom of heaven, when they think their pages are full of falsehoods on facts which they themselves have learnt from experience and the light of reason?[3]

Amen to that! Augustine is saying that we can and should accept the findings of reason and experience – what we now call science – and it is seriously damaging to the gospel to interpret the Scriptures so as to contradict these findings. Of course at the time of the scientific revolution thinkers such as Francis Bacon and Robert Boyle, who saw God as writing two books, nature and Scripture, realized that they could not contradict each other because they came from the same author. John Calvin realized that the Holy Spirit had accommodated himself to the understanding of the first readers of Scripture on matters of no importance to salvation, such as science. Thus Scripture was made accessible to all and Calvin said, "… he who would learn astronomy and other recondite arts, let him go elsewhere."[4]

Creation out of Nothing

We can see, then, that Genesis 1, at least, must be interpreted as making a theological rather than a scientific point. In fact, theologically one might immediately think there is a great consonance between Christian doctrine and what science is saying. We have seen how Augustine thought that time and space came into existence together. That is linked to the traditional doctrine of *creatio ex nihilo*, creation out of nothing. It is because God created out of nothing, and created freely and did not have to create, because God is self-sufficient in himself, that the universe is contingent. To say that the universe is contingent means that it need not have existed and could have been different from what it is.

This idea of the contingency of the universe is a very important consequence of the Christian doctrine of creation out of nothing. It was particularly important in motivating the development of modern science in Western Christendom since, if the universe could have been different from what it is, the only way to find out how it actually is is by experiment and observation. Sitting in one's armchair musing and using reason alone, in the manner of Plato, will not get us to scientific discovery; experiment and observation are essential.[5]

The doctrine of creation out of nothing stands in contrast to the pagan and Greek myths of creation. Many scholars believe that Genesis 1 stems from a priestly writer (the source "P") during the period of the Babylonian exile and is reacting against the Babylonian creation myth *Enuma Elish*. In this myth the earth and the heavens were made out of the divided corpse of an evil goddess destroyed in battle. Human beings were made from the blood of the evil goddess's consort in order to take over the heavy labour of the gods. Other ancient myths such as the earlier Babylonian *Atrahasis* epic tell a similar story and may also, or alternatively, have influenced the biblical writer.

The great Greek philosopher Plato was a bit more sophisticated than the Babylonians and in the *Timaeus* had the world made by the so-called "demiurge" or "craftsman". Crucially the demiurge did not create matter, but only moulded matter to form and shape the universe. In contrast to the Christian story as told in Genesis, this matter was resistant to the demiurge, and indeed the material world could not be said to be good on the Greek or any of the other pagan views.

Matter is denigrated in pagan views, but in Hebrew and Christian thought the material world is pronounced good by God. Very importantly, it is affirmed to be good by Christians on account of the incarnation, the fact that God took human flesh in Christ. But the main point I want to make here is that the Christian doctrine of creation can affirm that the creation is good because God made matter and did not just mould it. He made everything out of nothing.

As it happens, this doctrine of creation out of nothing is not totally clear from the Hebrew of Genesis 1:1. Indeed the interpretation of that verse is surprisingly controversial, although the goodness of creation is affirmed repeatedly in that chapter.

The first two verses of the Bible can be translated: "In the beginning when God created the heavens and the earth, the earth was without form and void." So the chapter may represent God as creating out of pre-existing chaos. Nevertheless, this chapter shows the effortless nature of the creation for God, who creates by simple command: God said, "Let there be... And it was so." There is no cosmic battle of gods; there is no *resistant* matter.

If the doctrine of creation out of nothing is not in Genesis then it is a later development. It is first found clearly in 2 Maccabees 7:28, which was written in the second century BC. The gruesome context is the arrest and torture by King Antiochus IV Epiphanes of a Hebrew mother and her seven sons for refusing to break the Mosaic law by eating pork. The mother of the Maccabean martyrs encourages the last of her sons to remain faithful in the face of torture with these words:

> I beseech you, my child, to look at the heaven and the earth and see everything that is in them, and recognize that God did not make them out of things that existed. Thus also mankind comes into being.

In the New Testament the clearest passages are:

> God... who gives life to the dead and calls into existence the things that do not exist. (Romans 4:17)

> By faith we understand that the world was created by the word of God, so that what is seen was made out of things which do not appear. (Hebrews 11:3)

Those great passages, which emphasize the role of the Son of God in creation, would also seem open to interpretation as indicating creation *ex nihilo*:

> ... all things were made through him and without him was not anything made that was made. (John 1:3)

> ... for in him all things were created, in heaven and on earth, visible and invisible, whether thrones or dominions or principalities or authorities – all things were created through him and for him. He is before all things, and in him all things hold together. (Colossians 1:16–17)

One of the earliest post-apostolic writings to assert *creatio ex nihilo* is *The Shepherd of Hermas*, dating probably from AD 140–155. While this is primarily a treatise about repentance and forgiveness, we do read the following about creation in its first commandment:

> First of all believe that there is one God who created and finished all things, and made all things out of nothing.[6]

Theophilus of Antioch (*c.*115–*c.*181) makes this definitive statement, noting that even humans can do what the Platonic demiurge can do, in utter contrast to what God can do:

> And what great thing is it if God made the world out of existent materials? For even a human artist, when he gets his material from some one, makes of it what he pleases. But the power of God is manifested in this, that out of things that are not He makes whatever He pleases...[7]

Irenaeus (*c*.130–*c*.200), Bishop of Lyons, cites the above passage from *The Shepherd of Hermas* as authority for his assertion of *creatio ex nihilo*. Irenaeus was a major opponent of the Gnostics, heretical groups who placed a complex system of emanations between the unknowable God and the demiurge who, as for Plato, created the material world. In contrast, Irenaeus insisted that God had no need of any intermediaries (he calls them angels) to create on his behalf. Rather, "with Him were always present the Word and Wisdom, the Son and the Spirit, by whom and in whom, freely and spontaneously, He made all things".[8] The doctrine of the Trinity is as yet undeveloped, although Irenaeus anticipates later orthodoxy, that Father, Son, and Holy Spirit, the three persons of the Godhead, are involved in creation.

The Dependence of the Universe on God

So *creatio ex nihilo* became fixed, and entered the creed. But back to the science for a moment. While the Big Bang theory seems to indicate a beginning in time, and the theorems of Vilenkin *et al.* seem to support a beginning, one needs to exercise caution in placing too much confidence in it. Fred Hoyle and his colleagues had atheistic ideological motivations for their steady-state theory, which proved to be wrong, but we must not be too smug. The Big Bang looks good for the Christian doctrine, but science has a habit of changing its mind and it can be dangerous to tie our theology too much to individual scientific theories. In contrast to Hoyle, the Christian priest Lemaître, "Father of the Big Bang", insisted that the Big Bang was a theory of cosmology with no theological implications. Indeed, as we saw in Chapter 2, he tried to dissuade the Pope on this point.

A major problem for physics is that the laws as we know them break down as you approach the beginning, time zero. A singularity of infinite density and zero size appearing in physics is an indication that new physics is required. There are candidate theories about an infinite universe and about infinitely many universes, which admittedly have many problems and, as we have

THE CHRISTIAN DOCTRINE OF CREATION

seen, still seem to indicate an absolute beginning. But perhaps cosmologists will eventually come up with a successful theory for an everlasting universe or a universe without a temporal beginning. Would that be a problem for theology?

When we examined Stephen Hawking's no boundary proposal we saw how he thinks there would be no need for God if his proposal were true. Another way of supposedly doing away with the need for God is said to be the spontaneous creation of the universe out of the so-called "quantum vacuum". This position is adopted by Hawking himself (in addition to the no boundary proposal), and most recently by cosmologist Lawrence Krauss.[9] In quantum theory the vacuum is not just empty space but a seething hive of activity with particles spontaneously coming into existence and then annihilating. In his book *A Universe from Nothing* Krauss redefines the notion of nothing so that the quantum vacuum can be identified with nothing. This really is sleight of hand. To philosophers "nothing" is the absence of anything. The quantum vacuum is a hive of activity with space acted on by quantum fields to produce particles and their anti-particles, and acted on by gravity. "Nothing" seems to be a very complicated something with all kinds of properties, including, Krauss says at one point, the property of being "unstable". And even if gravity were to do the trick because it has negative energy to cancel out positive matter energy, as is also claimed, we really would be entitled to ask where gravity came from in the first place.

Krauss *et al.* are as confused as the King in this incident from *Through the Looking Glass* (Figure 4.1):

> "I see nobody on the road," said Alice.
>
> "I only wish *I* had such eyes," the King remarked in a fretful tone. "To be able to see Nobody! And at that distance too!... Who did you pass on the road?" the King went on, holding out his hand to the Messenger...

"Nobody," said the Messenger.

"Quite right," said the King: "this young lady saw him too. So of course Nobody walks slower than you."

"I do my best," the Messenger said in a sulky tone. "I'm sure nobody walks much faster than I do!"

"He can't do that," said the King, "or else he'd have been here first."[10]

Figure 4.1 A recipe for confusion: the scene from *Through the Looking Glass* in which Alice sees "nobody" on the road.

Just as the King mistakes the absence of any person for a person called Nobody, so Krauss *et al.* ontologize the concept of "nothing", turning it from the absence of anything at all to a very sophisticated something.

Well, this nothing of Krauss, Hawking, and others is certainly not nothing in the sense that would trouble the theist.

These scientists simply have *not* proposed a model in which the universe arises spontaneously from literally nothing without the need for God.

Clearly the notion that the universe had a beginning is troublesome for atheists. However, even if any of their theories were true, Hawking, Krauss, and Hoyle before them would all be mistaken in seeing God as just the cause of a temporal beginning to the universe. The main lesson to draw from the doctrine of creation out of nothing is that the universe is totally dependent on God for its existence moment by moment, continuously. Furthermore, there is no resistant matter which is not under God's control.

Creation is not confined to, or even necessarily dependent on, a first moment. The doctrine of creation embraces the universe's dependence on God yesterday, today, and every day, not just at some moment 13.8 billion years ago. There is even some discussion in theological circles about whether creation is concerned at all with that first moment. Colin Gunton is one theologian who does think an actual beginning is important, nevertheless separates that theological question from the scientific story, as did Lemaître.[11] Others such as Janet Soskice and William Carroll emphasize the ontological dependence of all that is on God at every moment.[12]

In Scripture, Christ the Son of God is described as upholding the universe and sustaining it in being. God does not light the blue touch paper at the Big Bang and then absent himself ever after. Were he to cease upholding it, the universe would collapse into nothingness. No, God sustains the universe in being, through the Son according to Colossians and Hebrews (Colossians 1:17; Hebrews 1:3), and God interacts with his creation, bringing about his purposes within it. We might call this "continuing creation", *creatio continua*, not in the sense of Hoyle's scientific theory of continuous creation (the steady-state theory), though that would be compatible with it.

The idea that the universe would collapse into nothingness if God were to cease sustaining it in being is to be found in arguably the two greatest theologians of all time, St Augustine and St Thomas Aquinas. Here is what Augustine says:

> When a builder puts up a house, his work remains in spite of the fact that he is no longer there. But the universe will pass away in the twinkling of an eye if God withdraws his ruling hand.[13]

And here is St Thomas Aquinas, writing in the thirteenth century:

> For the *esse* [being] of all creaturely beings so depends upon God that they could not continue to exist even for a moment, but would fall away into nothingness unless they were sustained in existence by his power, as Gregory puts it.[14]

Furthermore, St Thomas recognized that God would be the cause of the universe's existence even if it had no beginning in time. He thought that it can be neither proved nor disproved that it had a beginning, but he himself believed it does from Genesis,[15] although, as we have seen, Genesis is not clear cut.

The Christian doctrine is much more correctly considered as an answer to the question "Why is there anything at all?" or "Why is there something rather than nothing?" than about the "how" of a temporal beginning.

That point can be seen in Thomas Aquinas's Five Ways.[16] These are five arguments for the existence of God, or really five variants of a single argument basically the idea that there must be a First Cause of all things. But it is quite clear that Aquinas means logical rather than temporal causality in this context. For Aquinas there can indeed be an infinite chain of causes going back in time, but that infinite chain needs a cause for its existence. And God provides the First Cause because he himself exists by necessity as I am about to explain. Aquinas did believe in a beginning of the universe, because that's how he read Scripture, but his argument is framed in logical, not temporal, terms.

Is God Needed as an Explanation?

The famous German theologian and martyr Dietrich Bonhoeffer reflected on the progress of science while imprisoned by the Gestapo. He wrote about how he thought the world was becoming autonomous, with no need for God. In particular he writes:

> It seems to me that in the natural sciences the process begins with Nicolas of Cusa and Giordano Bruno and the "heretical" doctrine of the infinity of the universe. The classical *cosmos* was finite, like the created world of the Middle Ages. An infinite universe, however it may be conceived, is self-subsisting, *etsi deus non daretur.* It is true that modern physics is not as sure as it was about the infinity of the universe, but it has not gone back to the earlier conceptions of its finitude.[17]

Bonhoeffer got this insight from reading the physicist Karl Friedrich von Weizsäcker's book *The World View of Physics.* Weizsäcker notes that Cardinal Nicolas of Cusa gets his view of the world as infinite from the idea that God infuses the world with as much of his own perfection as is possible while still making the world different from himself. The geometric symbol of God as the infinite sphere is transferred to the world as concretely imaging God. Two possible dangers identified by Weizsäcker are that the world becomes identified with God, or that God and the world become completely separate. Interestingly enough, some of the atheist scientists I have mentioned such as Hoyle and Krauss are happy enough with a concept of God that simply identifies God with the universe or with the laws of nature.

Bonhoeffer's point is more about the autonomy of the world, and certainly it is the case that we can do science *etsi deus non daretur* (as if God were not given). A major point Bonhoeffer makes, ahead of the better known statement of it by Christian physical chemist Charles Coulson in the 1950s, is that theology should not look for gaps in scientific explanation:

> It has again been brought home to me quite clearly how wrong it is to use God as a stop-gap for the incompleteness of our knowledge. If in fact the frontiers of knowledge are being pushed further and further back (and that is bound to be the case), then God is being pushed back with them, and is therefore continually in retreat. We are to find God in what we know, not in what we don't know; God wants us to realize his presence, not in unsolved problems but in those that are solved. That is true of the relationship between God and scientific knowledge, but it is also true of the wider human problems of death, suffering, and guilt... God is no stop-gap; he must be recognized at the centre of life, not when we are at the end of our resources.[18]

God is to be found in what we know and not in what we do not know. That is an important lesson for the modern "Intelligent Design" movement, which seeks precisely to locate God in gaps in the scientific story of biological evolution. Bonhoeffer says that this is a mistake in science and in other areas of human endeavour, and the answer is to place Christ at the centre rather than the margins of all we do.

I think there is some danger of treating the temporal beginning of the universe in cosmology as a "gap" in which to put God since it cannot yet be explained by science. The question is whether it is an ontological gap – one which is intrinsically inexplicable by science – or an epistemological gap, which merely reflects our current state of knowledge but in principle might be explained at some future point. The theorems of Vilenkin *et al.* seem to indicate an ontological gap, but I am still inclined to say that the argument of Craig and others should be construed as saying this makes God's existence likely or probable, rather than a deduction from pure logic.

But is Bonhoeffer right about an infinite universe, or its modern equivalent, a multiverse? Does the "autonomy" of an infinite universe imply there is no need for God to explain it? Would it make any difference if the universe were infinite in age and infinite in size? This brings me to the question of "ultimate explanation" since it seems to me that we can indeed do science, and find out about the universe, without reference to God, but that is a very different matter from saying that we can do without God as an explanation for the existence of the universe in the first place.[19]

Ultimate Explanations: Why is There Something Rather than Nothing?

By an ultimate explanation I mean an answer to the question "Why is there something rather than nothing?" or "Why is there any universe at all?" In their book, Stephen Hawking and Leonard Mlodinow claim that science can answer that question. How do they think this can be so?

The authors make a number of moves, which I shall now list. As you will see these are mainly philosophical assumptions, so once again it can hardly be said that philosophy is dead:

1. We create the history of the universe by observing it.[20]

2. All possible histories of the universe – ways of getting from state A to state B – are real, and we "select" a set of histories, no matter how improbable, that are compatible with our own existence.

3. Negative gravitational energy cancels out positive matter energy, which means the universe can create itself out of nothing.

4. M-theory (see pp. 79–80, and especially pp. 121–23)
   predicts that a great many universes were created out of
   nothing.

Add into this heady mix the no boundary proposal whereby time
becomes imaginary in the earliest epoch and you end up, say
Hawking and Mlodinow, with a universe that has no beginning
in time. Hence you avoid the need to invoke God to light the
blue touch paper to set it going, as we saw in the last chapter.

Point 1 in the above list arises from an extreme (philosophical!)
interpretation of quantum theory according to which reality is
"observer created". This idealist view gives consciousness pride
of place in bringing about reality through a kind of "backwards
causation". The physicist John Wheeler has proposed a view like
this which he calls "it from bit".[21] The reader may recall our
discussion of this in Chapter 2, and its similarity to a highly
speculative view of Fred Hoyle. A more recent supporter is Paul
Davies, who, like Hoyle, sees it as an alternative to invoking God
as Creator.[22] The universe exists as a kind of "self-excited circuit"
or self-subsistent "causal loop".

The reason for adopting this particular philosophical view
is that, according to quantum theory, the physical theory that
accurately describes the subatomic world, a system is in a mixture
(called a "superposition") of states until a measurement is made.
Then the system "collapses" to a single state.

It is, however, highly paradoxical to assert both that non-
conscious matter pre-exists and causes my existence and
that I cause its existence. And surely the result of a quantum
experiment, such as photons passing through two slits in a
screen, is decided by the imprint on the photographic plate
at the time the experiment happens, rather than by me three
months later when I take the plate out of the cupboard and
look at it![23] And even if we do ascribe creation of reality to
the human observer, this is far from "creation out of nothing"
since the superposition of states must have pre-existed the

observation. The reason for the existence of the self-excited circuit is not explained – and requires explanation for the same reason that the existence of anything at all requires explanation, as will become apparent shortly.

However, there is an interesting theological analogue to this "it from bit" idea. As noted by Barrow and Tipler,[24] this line of speculation can lead to the idea that all quantum events are coordinated by an Ultimate Observer who, by making the Final Observation, brings the whole universe into existence. This being would resemble the idealist Bishop Berkeley's picture of God, albeit a resemblance which Wheeler and others may well not welcome.[25]

The second philosophical assumption in the above list (that all possible histories of the universe are real and we "select" a set of histories compatible with our own existence) also arises from quantum theory. The great Nobel prize-winning physicist Richard Feynman showed that the probability of a quantum system going from state A to state B can be calculated mathematically by doing a weighted sum over all possible routes between A and B. This is Feynman's "sum-over-histories" approach to quantum theory. It is indeed a convenient mathematical calculating procedure. However, it gives no warrant for regarding all the histories as ontologically real. This is simply another paradoxical philosophical position adopted by Hawking and Mlodinow which we are free to reject. In any case we are free to reject the reality of multiple histories on the basis of Hawking and Mlodinow's own "model-dependent realism", according to that the only criterion is "usefulness" and it is pointless to ask whether a model is actually real!

What of the two remaining claims in the Hawking–Mlodinow list? They write: "M-theory predicts that a great many universes were created out of nothing. Their creation does not require the intervention of a supernatural being or god. Rather, these multiple universes arise naturally from physical law."[26] Again, this raises more questions than answers. First, there is no mention of the speculative nature of M-theory. M-theory is the overarching generalization of "string theory", a candidate theory to unite quantum theory and general relativity and to describe the universe in the first tiny fraction of a second of its existence. Hawking refers to M-theory as a network of different theories which apply to different situations, acceptable in model-dependent realism. What he does not mention is that serious questions have been raised over its lack of predictions and observational or experimental support. That goes particularly for the claim about many universes, which we shall return to in Chapters 7 and 8 (see especially pp. 121–23 for a fuller discussion of M-theory).

Secondly, the idea that the universe can create itself out of nothing is, of course, inherently self-contradictory. Apparently gravity can do the trick because its negative energy balances the positive energy needed to create matter. But suppose I take out a mortgage for £200,000 and purchase a house for £200,000. It could hardly be said that I had created something out of nothing. The fact that two quantities cancel out does not mean that something has popped into existence out of nothing. In his book *God, Chance and Necessity*, Keith Ward masterfully exposes the multiple fallacies involved in reifying "nothing" and ascribing all kinds of properties to "nothing" in the way that Hawking, Krauss, and others do, though Ward's target is the atheist physical chemist Peter Atkins.[27] As we saw above, this is just like the King in *Through the Looking Glass* mistaking nobody for a person called Nobody.

Contrary to what Hawking and Mlodinow say, their sleight of hand here does not mean that the universe creates itself out of nothing. If gravity and the laws of nature were responsible, one really would still be entitled to ask where these come from in the first place and where the quantum vacuum on which they act comes from. Hawking and Mlodinow state that invoking God here is to do no more than provide "a definition of God as the embodiment of the laws of nature".[28] But there is a world of difference between God as the supreme agent of creation, behind the laws, and the laws themselves, as I shall explain.

The fact is that only God can provide the ultimate explanation. No scientific theory can do that. The basic question is, "Why is there something rather than nothing? Why is there any universe at all?" God explains that. There is a universe because he freely created it. The theist would say that he wanted to bring about an environment in which free, rational creatures could flourish and have a relationship with him.

I am now going to utilize two important terms from philosophy, the terms "necessary" and "contingent". Something is said to be necessary if it cannot not exist and cannot be other than it is; as we have seen, something is contingent if it can be otherwise or if it need not exist at all.

Aquinas and many other theologians since have argued that it is the idea of God as "necessary being" which provides a stopping point for explanation. According to the above definition, to say that God is necessary means that he cannot but exist. He must exist. He cannot not exist. This is at least part of what the concept "God" means. Another way of saying it is that there is no possible universe in which God does not exist.

It follows from this that God was not himself created. He could not have been or else there would have been a time when God did not exist but something else did, namely whatever or whoever created God. Anything created is not God. Of course, someone could doubt that such a being exists – we know that many do doubt it – but it follows that if he does exist then he has always existed and will always exist and everything else that exists depends on him.

That is because everything else is "contingent". The word contingent means the opposite of necessary. Something which may or may not exist is contingent. It did not have to exist. It might not have existed.

Things are very different with the universe from the way they are with God. The universe might or might not have existed: it is contingent. Hawking put this very eloquently himself back in *A Brief History of Time*, when he wrote: "What is it that breathes fire into the equations, and makes a universe for them to describe?"[29] That is the fundamental question. Cosmologist Martin Rees recognizes that it cannot be answered by physics: "The pre-eminent mystery is why anything exists at all. What breathes life into the equations of physics, and actualized them in a real cosmos? Such questions lie beyond science, however: they are the province of philosophers and theologians."[30]

Interestingly the same point was made in 1978 by Dennis Sciama, who supervised the doctoral theses of both Hawking and Rees. I too had the privilege of being supervised by Sciama, who was a brilliant and inspiring cosmologist. Speaking as a scientist Sciama said this: "None of us can understand why there is a Universe at all, why anything should exist; that's the ultimate question."[31]

That's right. Science is powerless to explain why the universe exists. The universe cannot explain its own existence. It cannot create itself, by lifting itself up by its own bootstraps, as it were, into existence. You might have the most wonderful physical theory, the so-called "theory of everything" which unites all the forces of physics (it may even be M-theory!). But why there is a universe to which that theory applies is a question that science is simply powerless to answer. However, God, conceived as necessary being in the manner of Aquinas, does provide an explanation for the existence of the universe and for whatever physical theory applies to it.

To summarize, in answer to the question "Does a beginning require God?" we can say yes, and God would explain a beginning. We have now seen, however, that God is required regardless of whether the universe had a beginning. This is a rather more general form of the cosmological argument than the *kalām* argument favoured by William Lane Craig. God can create a universe with an infinite past if he so wishes, and God is required to explain the existence of the whole sequence of events, whether infinite in the past or not. It also seems to me to make no difference whatever if we speak of a multiverse or a single universe, a universe infinite in extent or one of finite size. A multiverse or an infinite universe requires just the same kind of explanation – why does it exist when it might well not have done? What breathes fire into the "multiverse generator", the set of equations that describes the multiverse?

The alternative is to give up on explanation. One would then simply have a universe (or multiverse) that is an unexplained contingent brute fact – and that ought to be deeply dissatisfying to any scientist, since scientists are generally motivated to find explanation and understanding. But now we need to go on and discuss the even more telling question: why does this particular universe exist? This is seemingly a very special universe, set up in a very special way. Why does the universe possess the laws and properties that it does, with the result that it is conducive to life? That is the subject of my next two chapters. We shall have cause to question the fifth claim of Stephen Hawking and Leonard Mlodinow in the first list I gave, at the beginning of Chapter 3, that a multiverse can provide the answer.

5

THE GOLDILOCKS ENIGMA

Life exists in the universe, only because the carbon atom
possesses certain exceptional properties.

Sir James Jeans (1930)[1]

Specialness of the Big Bang: Cosmic Fine-Tuning

We saw in Chapters 1 and 2 that the Big Bang is very well
supported by the evidence. Nevertheless the theory presents us
with some puzzles. It seems to be set up in a very special way
indeed, seemingly in order for us to be here to observe it. This
specialness relates to two areas:

1. The conditions right back at the beginning, shortly
   after the Big Bang, need to be just right to very high
   degrees of accuracy for the universe to give rise to life.

2. The constants that go into the laws of physics need to
   take the values they do, to significant accuracy, in order
   for the universe to give rise to life. These constants
   determine the relative strengths of the four fundamental
   forces of nature, namely gravity, the electromagnetic
   force, which holds atoms together, the weak nuclear
   force responsible for radioactive decay, and the strong
   nuclear force, which binds atomic nuclei together.
   They also include such quantities as the masses of

the fundamental particles. They determine how key physical processes go at different stages of the universe's evolution.

In the literature, the term "anthropic principle" is widely used to denote the constraints on the laws of nature and on the initial conditions at the Big Bang that are needed for our existence. The term is, however, rather problematic for several reasons. One reason is that, whereas the term anthropic is derived from the Greek *anthrōpos* (ἄνθρωπος) meaning "man", the conditions we are talking about are not the conditions required for specifically human life. More properly, we should speak of the conditions for intelligent life, or carbon-based life, to arise in the cosmos, though some of the conditions we are referring to are simply the conditions for anything interesting to arise in the universe at all. For these kinds of reasons, Paul Davies prefers the term "biophilic principle", meaning "life-friendly principle", to "anthropic principle". However, the latter term has stuck and I shall continue use it, or at least the word "anthropic", with suitable reservations.

A second reason for concern about the "anthropic principle" terminology is that it is ambiguous. There are several versions of the principle, so that the term can mean anything from a benign tautology to a highly speculative and dubious metaphysical claim. The "weak anthropic principle" (WAP) is stated as follows by John Barrow and Frank Tipler in their classic book on the subject:

> The observed values of all physical and cosmological quantities are not equally probable but they take on values restricted by the requirement that there exist sites where carbon-based life can evolve and by the requirement that the Universe be old enough for it to have already done so.[2]

Essentially this is saying that we can only measure the values of physical constants and cosmological quantities that are compatible with our own existence. In general, only a narrow range of values will be conducive to the development of life and clearly our measurements can only yield such values. The probabilities referred to are "posterior" probabilities or probabilities conditional on our existence. They are emphatically not a priori probabilities. This will be a key point in what is to come. Given that we exist, the constants must be highly constrained, but the more important question is: how likely is it that the constants take those values in the first place so as to make possible our existence?

The weak anthropic principle is a tautology. However, it raises the issue as to whether there are other parts of the universe, or indeed other universes, in which the physical parameters take on different values and where carbon-based life could not exist. Indeed the WAP is often interpreted to mean that there are indeed other such universes or universe regions, and our measurements are simply the result of an "observer selection effect" in that we could not measure alternative values. I shall return to this important point in more detail in Chapter 8.

More speculative is the strong anthropic principle (SAP), defined by Barrow and Tipler as follows:

> The Universe must have those properties which allow life to develop within it at some stage in its history.[3]

If one takes this statement at face value it is very hard to see its justification. A priori, why should the universe not be lifeless? Can universes described by different parameters from those we observe not exist? It would seem that the only way to make sense of the SAP is to interpret it as asserting "observer created reality", i.e. the idea that we bring about the universe's existence by observing it. This is the interpretation of quantum theory we met when discussing Hawking and Mlodinow in Chapter 4, and we have seen that variants of it have been adopted at different times by Fred Hoyle, John Wheeler, and Paul Davies. The SAP then transmutes into what Barrow and Tipler dub the "participatory anthropic principle" (PAP), and we have already seen that this idea is both paradoxical and unnecessary.

Twelve Examples of Cosmic Fine-Tuning[4]

There are many, many examples of this so-called fine-tuning, and the following is a selection of them, which shows the basic idea:

1. The mean density of matter–energy in the universe

The mean density of matter–energy in the universe has to be just right in order for life to arise in the universe. In Chapter 1 we saw that there are three regimes for the curvature of space–time: positive, negative, and zero (flat). Which pertains depends on the mean density, and there is a critical value of mean density above which the universe will be positively curved, below which it will be negatively curved, and equal to which it will be flat. Today the mean density is very close to the critical value and that implies that it was much, much closer at the earliest times.

As I mentioned in Chapter 1, cosmologists define the parameter Ω (omega) to be the mean density divided by the critical value. As we saw, the mean density, and therefore Ω as well, comprises three components, due to radiation, matter, and the cosmological constant. The value of Ω today, denoted by Ω_0, has been estimated with remarkable precision from observations from the WMAP (Wilkinson Microwave Anisotropy Probe) satellite and the more recent Planck satellite. The radiation component of Ω_0 is negligible, the contribution due to matter is about 0.32, and that due to the cosmological constant, which can be regarded as equivalent to a density, is about 0.68. So the combined value is very close to 1.

In the early universe the radiation component would have dominated up until the crossover point, at which the two densities had decreased to the same value. This was when the universe was about 50,000 years old;[5] after this, the matter component took over. Only in the recent history of the universe has Λ, the cosmological constant component, started to dominate, because the density corresponding to Λ is constant whereas the matter density decreases with the expansion. It should also be noted that, of the matter component, ordinary matter contributes only 0.05 to Ω_0 and a mysterious "dark matter" comprises the other 0.27. We know that dark matter exists because gravity would be insufficient to stop galaxies flying apart without it, yet we do not know what this dark matter is.

Now to the crux of the matter. Suppose we think of the state of the universe about one second after the Big Bang. The physics at this early epoch is surprisingly well known. In order for galaxies to form a few hundred thousand years later, at that very early time the universe needs to be expanding at just the right rate to a high degree of accuracy. If the expansion rate is too small, the density will be higher than the critical value by too large an amount, gravity will pull the universe back, and recollapse will occur before galaxies have had a chance to form. If the expansion rate is too large, the density will be lower than the critical value by too much, and gravity will be insufficient for inhomogeneities (regions of small excess density) to condense to form galaxies. In fact, one second after the Big Bang, Ω needs to be equal to 1 to within an error of 10^{-15}. In this scientific index notation 10^{15} means 1 with 15 noughts after it and 10^{-15} is 1 divided by 10^{15}. Hence in normal decimal notation Ω must be less than 1.000000000000001 and greater than 0.999999999999999. This translates into even more prodigious accuracy the further back we go in time towards the origin. Of course the physics is much less secure, but suppose we straightforwardly project back our models to the earliest point we can speak of sensibly at all, namely 10^{-43} seconds from the origin, when an as yet unknown theory of quantum gravity is required (though for which M-theory is a candidate). At that point Ω needs to be equal to 1 to within an error of 10^{-60}, i.e. 1 part in 10^{60}. An accuracy of one part in 10^{60} is that required to aim a gun at a coin 13 billion light years away at the opposite end of the universe and hit it.

Scientific notation

Readers may be familiar with scientific notation from school mathematics, for example that x^2 means x multiplied by itself. By extension x^n means x multiplied by itself n times, i.e. $x \times x \times x \ldots \times x$ with n xs in the calculation. x^{-n} means $1/x^n$, i.e. 1 divided by x^n. This provides a convenient way of expressing large numbers as powers of 10 and small numbers as negative powers of 10. Thus, as noted in the text, 10^{15} is 1,000,000,000,000,000 (1 with 15 noughts after it, and 10^{-15} is 1 divided by 1,000,000,000,000,000, i.e. 0.000000000000001 (14 noughts altogether).

It may be that the closeness of Ω to 1 may be explicable in terms of a more fundamental theory operating at the earliest times, namely the popular theory known as "inflation". We shall consider inflation in a little more detail in Chapter 7. However, this would merely push back the specialness of the initial conditions onto the theory that produced those conditions at ultra-early times, a point we consider in Chapter 6.

2. The size of the universe

Related to the above, and contrary to our intuitions, it turns out that the universe needs to be the vast size it is in order for humankind to exist.[6] This is the size reached by an expanding universe, with density close to the critical value, in the 13.8 billion years it takes to evolve human beings. In the simplest cosmological model, the flat universe with zero cosmological constant – and this is accurate enough for the present purpose – the size, mass, and age of the observable universe are connected by a simple formula. An expanding universe with the mass of a single galaxy has enough matter to make 100 billion stars like the sun, but such a universe would have expanded for only about a month so that no stars could have formed in fact.[7] Thus the argument that the vastness of the universe points to human *insignificance* is turned on its head – in reality only if it is so vast, containing 100 billion galaxies, could we be here! The universe needs to be about as old as it is, and therefore as large as it is, for stars to have manufactured the chemical elements necessary for life. On the other hand, it could not be too much older since in that case all the stars would have died out.[8] This is clearly in line with the WAP as defined above: we could not arise earlier or later in the universe's history. Nevertheless, it does seem to turn on its head the oft-repeated argument that we are an insignificant speck in a gigantic cosmos: only if the universe is so enormous could we exist at all.

3. Helium production in the Big Bang

One of the most important elements necessary for life, certainly life as we know it, is hydrogen: no hydrogen means no water and hence no life. In Chapter 2 we saw how helium was produced from hydrogen in the Big Bang. If the weak nuclear force, the force responsible for radioactive decay, were not, apparently accidentally, related to the gravitational force in a rather special way, either all the hydrogen would be converted to helium within the first three minutes of the Big Bang or none would be. In the former case, with the weak force somewhat weaker, one would end up with no possibility of water or life at any subsequent stage in the universe's history. Bernard Carr also notes that helium burning stars may not be long-lived enough for life to develop even if it could.[9] Moreover, the requirement that massive stars explode in supernovae, to release the chemical elements they have manufactured, constrains the relationship between the weak force and gravity in both directions.

4. Proton–electron mass ratio

The mass of the proton must be almost exactly 1,837 times the mass of the electron, as it is, for the possibility of interesting chemicals to be made and to be stable, certainly for complicated molecules like DNA, which are the building blocks of life.[10]

5. The Hoyle resonance

One of the most famous examples of fine-tuning is that discovered by Fred Hoyle, which I discussed in Chapter 2. The ratio of two of the fundamental forces of nature – the strong nuclear force, which binds atomic nuclei together, and the electromagnetic force, which operates between charged particles – has to be just right for carbon and oxygen to be made inside stars. The value it takes ensures that there is a "resonance" in the carbon atom at the right level to make carbon production efficient, but no resonance at a level in the oxygen atom that would make all the carbon turn into oxygen. It is worth repeating Hoyle's comment here, when he made this discovery, that "a superintellect has monkeyed with physics, as well as with chemistry and biology, and that there are no blind forces worth speaking about in nature". It is very significant that this is a man who earlier in his life described religion as an illusion.

6. The cosmological constant

Possibly the most outstanding problem in cosmology is the fine-tuning of the cosmological constant, Λ. As mentioned in Chapter 1, the 2011 Nobel prize went to two teams of astronomers who discovered that Λ is positive. In fact, half went to Saul Perlmutter of the Lawrence Berkeley National Laboratory in California, and half to Brian Schmidt of the Australian National University and Adam Riess of Johns Hopkins University, Baltimore. The upshot of this discovery is that Einstein was wrong to reject Λ on aesthetic grounds and Lemaître was right to keep it.

The problem the observations pose is that the observed value of Λ is very small. Physicists think they know where Λ comes from. As we have seen, in quantum theory the vacuum is not empty but a hive of constantly fluctuating activity, and possesses energy. Λ is believed to be the energy of the vacuum, and it has been called "dark energy". The unfortunate thing is that when Λ is calculated it gives a value 10^{120} times that which is compatible with observations. If Λ really took the calculated value, you would be pulled apart in an instant with your body parts flying away to the ends of the universe (Figure 5.1). (Of course, if this were so, no galaxies and stars, let alone yourself, could have come into existence in the first place!) One way of putting the problem is to say that there needs to be another component (the "Einstein component") of Λ, which almost exactly cancels the vacuum energy. This Einstein component must be the same as the vacuum energy component in its first 120 digits. This is a truly stunning example of fine-tuning.

Figure 5.1 If the cosmological constant took the calculated value, the consequences would be devastating.

7. The initial entropy of the universe

Sir Roger Penrose, Emeritus Rouse Ball Professor of Mathematics at Oxford and outstanding cosmologist, has considered the amount of order there was at the beginning of the universe. Order is measured by a quantity called entropy, and, as systems become more disorderly over time, entropy increases. This is the "second law of thermodynamics" and is related to the familiar arrow of time. If I knock my coffee cup off the table, the cup will smash and the coffee will cool and diffuse through the carpet. Shards of china and cool, diffused coffee do not magically come together again and jump onto tables as pristine cups of hot coffee. If you see such a sequence on your TV screen, you immediately realize that you are either in the world of Harry Potter or someone is playing a recording backwards. The true "arrow of time" is in the direction of increasing disorder.

Penrose puts it like this concerning the entropy of the universe. He says that the Creator had something like $10^{10^{123}}$ possible universe configurations to choose from, only one of which would have the order which ours does.[11] Remember that 10^{123} is 1 with 123 noughts after it; $10^{10^{123}}$ is 1 with 10^{123} noughts after it! That is the order necessary to produce a cosmos with all the galaxies, stars, and planets that our universe possesses. This looks like the most astonishing fine-tuning of all since, as Penrose says, if one wanted to write this number out in full by writing a nought on every atom in the universe this would be impossible since there are a mere 10^{80} atoms in the entire observable universe. There is a twist in the tale which makes it even more remarkable and seriously problematic for the multiverse explanation of fine-tuning, but consideration of that must wait until Chapter 8.

8. The dimensionality of space

We inhabit a universe with three space dimensions and one of time, and it might seem strange even to question whether the dimensionality of the universe could be different. It might also seem strange to call dimensionality a "physical" constant, but mathematicians happily play with multidimensional spaces, and even some physical theories now incorporate more than the usual three space dimensions.

In M-theory, the generalization of string theory favoured by Stephen Hawking, there are believed to be ten dimensions of space and time embedded in a further dimension, making eleven dimensions in all. It is further claimed, rather conveniently, that all but three space dimensions, and the one of time, are curled up ("compactified") so as to be very, very tiny and below any observational threshold.

Analogously with other cases of fine-tuning, it turns out that life can only exist in a three-dimensional space (or one in which other dimensions are negligible). As both Rees and Hawking note, digestion would be rather difficult for a two-dimensional creature since its digestive tract would split the animal in two![12] Obviously the possibilities for complex structure would be even more limited in only one dimension. Moreover, only in three dimensions is there an inverse square law of gravitation, and this turns out to be the only law giving stable planetary orbits. For example, in four dimensions the law would have to be inverse cube, and this would not permit a stable solar system. Indeed, this fact was noted as evidence of design by Archdeacon William Paley in his treatise *Natural Theology* of 1802.[13] Paley is remembered especially for his famous parable about finding a watch on a heath and inferring that it was designed, and arguing analogously for the design of the much more complex eye observing the watch. That kind of design argument, relating to separate design of individual structures within nature, is commonly thought to have been defeated by Darwinism, which can explain how such structures came about through the process of evolution. However, the more general argument relating to the laws of nature themselves, which give rise to the order that we see, is unaffected by Darwinism. So, regarding the latter, why there are three dimensions of space, or why there is a compactification mechanism which reduces higher dimensions to minuscule proportions, remains a valid question.

It is worth noting that the same comments apply to the inverse square law of attraction between protons and electrons in atoms, so unless space had three dimensions not even atoms would be stable![14] Evidently three spatial dimensions are an essential requirement if the universe is to be life-bearing.

9. Magnitude of density fluctuations

The universe needs to be smooth and uniform in its distribution of mass, but not too uniform ("homogeneous"). Galaxy formation relies on the existence of slight density contrasts in the expanding universe so that gravitational collapse can occur. If these "density perturbations" are much less than about 1 part in 10^5 at the time of recombination, when the interactions between matter and radiation cease, then they will not amplify to form galaxies. If they are too large at this time (say 1 part in 100 or more), they will collapse prematurely into black holes. In fact, the WMAP satellite shows the value of the density perturbations to be about 1 in 10^5, making galaxy formation just viable (thankfully!). Like the overall density of mass–energy, the imprinting of inhomogeneities of the right magnitude may ultimately be explicable in terms of a more fundamental theory, notably "inflation" (for which, see Chapter 7). However, again as in the case of mean density, this would simply push back the fine-tuning of the initial conditions of the universe onto the theory which supposedly applies at ultra-early times (see Chapter 6 for more on this recurring point).[15]

10. Getting the right kinds of stars

The strength of the gravitational force needs to be related to that of the electromagnetic force in a rather special way, and changing either force by a small amount would have dramatic consequences on this relationship.[16] The practical outcome would be a severe restriction on the types of star which can occur.[17] If gravity were slightly stronger, or electromagnetism slightly weaker, all stars would be blue giants, which are substantially larger than the sun and much hotter. If it were the other way round and gravity were slightly weaker, or electromagnetism slightly stronger, all stars would be red dwarfs, which are small and cool objects by stellar standards. As it is, most stars are like our sun, lying between these extremes.

It is not clear that red dwarfs could generate enough heat to foster life on their planets, but in any case they would never explode in supernovae, as required for the dissemination of the chemical elements that are the building blocks of life. On the other hand, Brandon Carter, originator of the "anthropic principle" terminology, has speculated that blue stars, which radiate rather than convect heat, and which retain strong rates of spin on their axes, might not have planets (he believes that a star's surface convection is important for planetary formation). In any case they would be much shorter lived, and so there would be much less time for life on any planets to get going. As Davies points out, what is clear is that this small change would give rise to a radically different universe.[18]

11. The strength of gravity

An even more serious constraint on the gravitational force is noted by the philosopher Robin Collins;[19] Astronomer Royal Lord (Martin) Rees makes similar points.[20] Collins argues that the probability that intelligent life could arise would be dramatically reduced if the strength of gravity were more than about 3,000 times the actual value that it takes in our universe. By comparison the range that permits a universe at all is something like 0 to 10^{40} times the actual value (the latter would make gravity equal in strength to the strong nuclear force, the strongest of nature's four forces). An increase in the strength of gravity by a factor of a billion would imply that any land animal the size of humans would be crushed; even insects would require thick legs to support them and no animals could grow much bigger. To compensate for this by reducing the size of the planet, so that the planet's gravity were only 1,000 times that of earth – still marginal for the possibility of organisms with a brain size comparable to ours – would imply a planetary diameter of about 40 feet, utterly insufficient to sustain the appropriate ecological environment. If gravity were multiplied by the factor of 3,000, planets could not last for more than a billion years, giving insufficient time for intelligent life to arise. Dividing 3,000 by the possible maximum value of 10^{40} yields a tiny probability of 3×10^{-37} for gravity to be fine-tuned.

12. The excess of matter over anti-matter

In its earliest moments the universe was endowed with a very small excess of matter particles (such as protons, neutrons, and electrons) over their corresponding anti-matter particles (such as anti-protons, anti-neutrons, and positrons). This excess amounted to 1 particle in 10^9. Matter particles and their anti-particles have opposite charge and annihilate to give photons of radiation. (For the puzzled reader, the neutron has no net charge but consists of three charged constituent particles called "quarks" whose total charge sums to zero; the anti-neutron consists of the three corresponding charged anti-quarks. Protons also consist of three quarks, but their total charge is positive.)

The problem is that if the universe contained an equal number of matter and anti-matter particles, there would be insufficient matter following annihilation for galaxies to form. The process of cosmic evolution – galaxies, stars, planets, life – would not even get going. While it may be the case that some more fundamental theory operating at the earliest epoch (a Grand Unified Theory) may eventually be able to show how this imbalance between matter and anti-matter arises, all this would do, yet again, would be to push the problem back a stage, from the fine-tuned excess of matter over anti-matter to the theory which produces the imbalance.

As I say, there are a host of these examples of fine-tuning and I have mentioned just a few of the most significant. John Leslie in his excellent little book *Universes* lists many more,[21] which makes one wonder whether the number of constraints might not be greater than the number of constants and therefore render it quite remarkable that any set of life-conducive parameters exists at all – another point we return to in Chapter 6.

Alister McGrath also notes a number of anthropic properties that come into play as life develops. A significant example would be the remarkable chemical properties of water. For example, the fact that ice floats on water means that in cold environments there is often liquid water below solid water, so fish can survive even when a lake has frozen over. Water also possesses important solvent properties, which are necessary for life since many biochemical reactions only take place in solution.[22]

We saw in the last chapter that the universe itself needs explanation, whether or not it has a beginning in time, and, if as appears to be the case it does have a beginning in time, we have seen how that poses a particular problem for atheism. On the face of it, it looks as though something is going on with regard to the fine-tuning and as if this too requires explanation. The cosmologist Paul Davies puts it like this: "Like the porridge in the tale of Goldilocks and the three bears, the universe seems to be 'just right' for life, in so many intriguing ways."[23]

Figure 5.2 Baby bear's porridge was "just right".

Davies agrees that an explanation is required, but this is something some other physicists and philosophers have denied. Hence, in the next chapter, we first consider whether indeed an explanation for the fine-tuning is required, before going on to examine what explanations are on offer.

6

EXPLAINING THE FINE-TUNING

You find it surprising that I think of the comprehensibility of the world (in so far as we are entitled to speak of such a comprehensibility) as a miracle or an eternal mystery. But surely, *a priori*, one should expect the world to be chaotic, not to be grasped by thought in any way. One might (indeed one *should*) expect that the world evidence itself as lawful only so far as we impose an order. This would be a sort of order like the alphabetical order of words in a language. On the other hand, the kind of order created, for example, by Newton's gravitational theory is of a very different character. Even if the axioms of the theory are posited by man, the success of such a procedure supposes in the objective world a high degree of order which we are in no way entitled to expect *a priori*. Therein lies the "miracle" which becomes more and more evident as our knowledge develops.

Albert Einstein[1]

Is There Really Anything to Explain?[2]

Some philosophers and physicists have argued along the following lines. We inhabit this particular universe with the apparently fine-tuned features described. If these features were not as they are, we would not be here to observe them. We *can only* observe a universe that gives rise to our own existence (as the weak anthropic principle asserts). It follows that we should not be surprised to observe fine-tuned parameters that necessarily have to be as they are in order for us to exist in the first place. Every possible combination of parameters has a tiny probability of being chosen on a random basis to describe a universe, and we simply shouldn't be surprised at the set of parameters that does apply to our universe.

Nobel prize-winning physicist Richard Feynman once gave a public lecture, during which he described how, on the way in to the lecture, he had observed a car in the car park with Tennessee number plate ARW 357.[3] "Can you imagine? Of all the millions of license plates in the state, what was the chance I would see that particular one tonight? Amazing!" remarks Feynman. Of course, the a priori probability is very small, but this causes Feynman no problem, because any other car would be just as unlikely and just as insignificant. It just so happens that the car with number plate ARW 357 was the one that showed up. Similarly, according to some physicists, we do indeed live in a universe in which the laws of physics are ordered in a particular way, but if they were different in any number of equally improbable ways, we would not be here. Some cosmologists and philosophers believe that life is insignificant, a bit of froth on the surface of a meaningless universe, in which case alternative universes are just like alternative cars showing up in the car park.

This argument is open to serious challenge. For a start, we could tweak the story a little. I have a friend whose initials are ARW and who was born in March 1957. My friend collects classic cars and purchases number plates with his initials on them. If a classic car with number plate ARW 357 turned up outside my house, it would be very significant, indicating that my friend was visiting. What appeared a random choice of number would be transformed into one of real significance.

Surely most of us would regard life, and in particular our own existence, not as mere froth on the surface of the universe but as of real significance and value. For this reason, the universe that actually exists is in a different category from the vast majority of universes which do not possess this value. Furthermore, we can provide an explanation, namely the theistic hypothesis, for why, of the vastly many universes which could exist, one of meaning and value actually does so. Surely this explanation is much more likely to be true than mere random choice from the set of possible universes.

Richard Swinburne gives an example which provides a good counter to the "car park argument".[4] A madman operates a machine that shuffles ten packs of cards simultaneously. He tells his kidnapped victim that unless the machine produces, and continues to produce for every draw of cards, ten aces, the machine will explode so that the victim will be killed and no longer able to observe any draws. But when the victim does observe successive draws, his conclusion is surely that the machine is rigged, rather than that there is nothing to explain, because he wouldn't be around if anything else but ten aces were drawn, and this is no more unlikely than any other draw.

John Leslie has a similar example, which also brings out the fallacy of thinking that, because we can only observe "our" set of parameters, the need for explanation is thereby removed. A firing squad of 50 sharpshooters is lined up against me (Figure 6.1). If they all miss, it is surely inadequate simply to shrug my shoulders and reply, "If they hadn't all missed, then I shouldn't be considering the affair."[5] My still being alive requires explanation – either the sharpshooters all deliberately missed or, perhaps, "immensely many firing squads are at work and I'm among the very rare survivors." We consider the latter possibility, which corresponds to the many universes hypothesis, below. Here we note that this brings out a point made earlier when discussing the WAP. Given that I am here to tell the tale, the (posterior) probability that the sharpshooters all missed is 1 (they certainly had to), but the prior probability that they would all miss, on the basis of random chance, is very low indeed. The fact that they did so has a better explanation than chance, namely they all deliberately missed. I actually doubt whether invoking a huge ensemble of firing squads around the universe makes any difference to *my* survival, but that I think is where there is a disanalogy between multiple firing squads and a multiverse.

Figure 6.1 Will all the members of the firing squad miss?

As yet another example, suppose I shuffle a pack of cards and deal them out before you. Suppose that they come out in the order Ace, Two, Three… up to King of Clubs, then the same for Diamonds, Hearts, and Spades. This hand is in fact just as improbable as any other. Indeed it has a chance of about 1 in 10^{68} of occurring. It seems to me, however, that there is a better explanation in this case than just sheer luck. If I were a card sharp, you would not be the least surprised that I could produce such a hand, and you would be more rational to suppose that I am a card sharp than to believe the outcome was entirely due to chance.

The difference between the hand dealt and the vast majority of other hands is that this one is meaningful – indeed it displays a perfect pattern. Hence, it makes sense to look for an explanation beyond mere randomness. Added to which, there is a straightforward explanation available.

It is similar with the universe. This is not just "any old universe". The vast majority of universe configurations obtained by changing the parameters by the smallest amount are completely dead and boring. They are almost entirely devoid of meaning and value. This universe is shot through with meaning and value because, at least in one small part of it, it has produced creatures with rational powers to understand it and appreciate its beauty, and the capacity to exercise moral responsibility. The universe has in a sense "become aware of itself". Moreover, many scientists see objective value exhibited in the universe, for example Paul Davies, who writes:

> My own inclination is to suppose that qualities such as ingenuity, economy, beauty, and so on have a genuine transcendent reality – they are not merely the product of human experience – and that these qualities are reflected in the structure of the natural world.[6]

Possible Explanations for the Fine-Tuning

This specialness of the universe, which is essential if there is to be life, just cries out for explanation. The most obvious explanation is that it was made that way; it was designed so that life would appear. Christians would say that God intended there to be living creatures with the capacity for reason and with free will, who would be able to have a relationship with him. It should be recognized, however, that this explanation is very different from the design arguments in biology put forward by the so-called "Intelligent Design" movement. Here we are talking about why the laws of physics and the initial conditions to which they are applied are as they are. We are emphatically not looking for explanatory gaps in the processes described by these laws when they are applied, as Intelligent Design proponents do, but addressing the metascientific question, "Why do the laws take the particular form they do?" This is not a question normally addressed by science, and indeed I would argue is beyond science's power to explain. No, physicists discover what the laws are and, from the laws and initial conditions of a system, work out how that system behaves. The question as to why the laws are as they are takes us beyond physics to metaphysics.

Many scientists, however, regard any kind of design hypothesis with loathing. They want to restrict their explanations, even for why the laws of physics are as they are, to within science itself.

So what alternatives have scientists come up with? I am going to contrast two strategies that scientists have pursued in order to avoid the implication of design by God.

1. The first is to seek an explanation from within science for the values taken by the various constants of physics – to derive them from some more fundamental theory, and ultimately from a so-called "theory of everything" (TOE). The argument states that we might be wrong in thinking that the constants etc. could take different values from those they do in fact take. In reality, the argument goes, they could not be different from what they are, and so the whole anthropic edifice is built on a mistake. Interestingly Einstein spent his later years in a fruitless search for a theory like this: "What I am really interested in is whether God could have made the world in a different way," he said – although this quotation obviously indicates that he still saw no contradiction with God being behind it. Similarly Sir Arthur Eddington also spent the latter part of his career in a fruitless search for what he called a "fundamental theory" – and Eddington as a Quaker also believed in God.

   Connected with this search for a TOE, though different from it, is the aim to show that the initial conditions are not special: to argue that whatever they were, the universe would turn out much the same. Ernan McMullin has described this latter position as the "indifference principle" in cosmology.[7] It is another grand philosophical principle, like the perfect cosmological principle we met in Chapter 1, which is not demanded by the science but enables those who adopt it to avoid the need for a designer to choose the initial conditions.

2. The second strategy is diametrically opposed to this. As intimated above, it is to postulate a multiverse. A multiverse is a vast, usually infinite, set of existent universes, embracing the whole range of values of the constants and initial conditions. The idea is that if a multiverse exists you can then say: Hey presto! Given the vast ensemble, our universe with its suite of parameters is bound to exist, and we should not be surprised to find ourselves in it, because we simply could not exist in the overwhelming majority of universes that differ from ours in their parameter values to the slightest degree.

Let me remind the reader that, from our discussion in Chapter 4, neither of these strategies explains why anything exists, why there is a universe at all. However, each does attempt to explain why the universe is like it is, given that it exists.

Atheist strategy (1)

Strategy (1) can be further divided into two distinct versions. In the first version, the constants can be derived from a more fundamental theory, but it is still the case that alternative theories exist and could apply to alternative universes. In that case the basic problem remains. The question "Why do the constants take the values they do?" is simply modified to "Why does this particular theory of everything (TOE), which gives rise to just the right values for the constants, and hence to life, apply? Why is this particular TOE put into effect in a universe?"

The second version is much more radical and makes a much bolder metaphysical claim. This is that there is only one self-consistent set of physical laws, and the constants pertaining in these laws necessarily take the values they do – they are calculated from the one and only self-consistent TOE. Thus the universe could not have been different, so, with the big proviso that it exists, then it is necessarily the way it is – and that is because the TOE is taken to comprise the only self-consistent theory and set of parameters there is.

If that is so, there is still a massive puzzle because we can now ask, "Why does the only self-consistent set of physical laws give rise to life?" It could have given rise to an isolated amorphous lump of rock and nothing else, or to just a few scattered particles in otherwise empty space. Why on earth did it give rise to a universe with all the rich complexity including living creatures that we see? Given the infinite variety of outcomes we can imagine, it is desperately puzzling why the only possible set of laws gives a universe with human beings in it.

The philosopher Peter van Inwagen gives a helpful analogy.[8] Imagine a $1,000 \times 1,000$ square grid. Write the first million digits of the number π, familiar from school mathematics as the ratio of the circumference to the diameter of a circle, consecutively into the grid. Then colour the grid by assigning a different colour to each of the digits 0, 1, 2, 3... 9. Now suppose that the result is a painting of surpassing beauty, something like the Mona Lisa. That would be utterly astonishing. But the picture is necessarily what it is because the digits of π are necessarily what they are. Nevertheless, it would still be immensely surprising if the Mona Lisa rather than an amorphous mess emerged from this process. Of course, given that the digits of π never repeat, there will be some sequence of a million digits way down the line which yields a beautiful pattern, but if the first million did so, that would be utterly amazing.

The atheist physicist Victor Stenger has proposed a variant of strategy (1), with two parts to it.[9] First, Stenger sees the laws of physics as necessary – that is, they comprise the only self-consistent set of laws there could be. Secondly, he thinks the parameters of physics are not really fine-tuned anyway, or at least vastly less finely-tuned than has been thought hitherto. Science itself can explain the fine-tuning.

Stenger's arguments are open to the above objection concerning the sheer astonishment that a universe with the order and structure ours has should be the only possible universe. Moreover, Stenger's ideas have been critiqued in considerable detail by astronomer Luke Barnes[10] and by philosopher Robin Collins.[11] Collins has in fact made an important contribution to the whole discussion of fine-tuning which we shall return to in Chapter 8: he makes the point, diametrically opposed to Stenger, that the universe is *extra-specially* fine-tuned for embodied conscious agents (ECAs) like ourselves. Both Barnes and Collins find Stenger's position seriously flawed, which is not surprising since the one thing that is generally agreed upon in cosmology is the existence of the fine-tuning – however much difference there might be in preferred explanations for it.

In order to claim that the laws of physics are necessary, Stenger argues that any objective laws applying to a universe must possess certain symmetries and be "point-of-view invariant"; that is, they must not depend on the reference frame of the observer. But as Barnes points out, which symmetries apply to the universe is a matter for discovery, not armchair theorizing. Indeed any physical theory could be written in point-of-view invariant form, so that point-of-view invariance tells us nothing about what physical theory actually applies.

In any case, symmetries must be broken in order for anything complex to arise in the universe. For example, the pure FLRW (Friedmann–Lemaître–Robertson–Walker) cosmological models described in Chapter 1, which are perfectly symmetric, can only be an approximation to the real world. If these models provided an exact description of the universe, it would be perfectly homogeneous and isotropic, looking identical in all places and all directions, and there would be no possibility of any complex structures arising. Precisely how the symmetries are broken is critical to the prospect for life in the universe. Mere random symmetry-breaking, which Stenger thinks will do the trick, is, on the contrary, most unlikely to produce a universe just right for life. This is why many physicists, unlike Stenger, think a multiverse, in which symmetries are broken in all possible ways, is necessary to avoid divine design.

Stenger argues, for example, that gravity is a necessary property of the universe. He agrees with Collins that a universe without gravity could not support life (because matter would not clump together to form stars), but argues that such a universe could not exist. To this, Collins points out, quite simply, that the gravitational constant could be put to zero and hence one could very easily have a universe without gravity. It would seem that Stenger has a rather stunted imagination of what kinds of universe could possibly exist.

Stenger also denies that the strength of gravity is fine-tuned. He says that the strength of the gravitational force could be defined in terms of the masses of elementary particles and therefore would not be fine-tuned. But, as Collins points out, that doesn't alter the need for fine-tuning, only whether one calls it fine-tuning or the strength of gravity! Collins reiterates the points that I gave in Chapter 5. Indeed he argues that the strength of gravity is not just fine-tuned for embodied conscious agents (ECAs) but ultra fine-tuned for them to be able to develop civilization – build houses, forge metal, etc. An increase in the strength of gravity by a factor of only 100 (that is, much less than the factor of 3,000 he considered earlier) would make this impossible. We come back to Collins' point about ultra fine-tuning in Chapter 8.

Collins also refers to the fine-tuning of the cosmological constant Λ. He says it is difficult to see how any more fundamental law, as Stenger postulates, could require it to be very small, as it is found to be. There are numerous problems with this idea, not least that it contradicts the fact that Λ is required to be large in the very early universe if inflation (widely accepted by cosmologists, though Collins thinks still speculative) is to occur. And even if there were such a more fundamental law, the problem that one has simply transferred the fine-tuning of the constant into the law remains – and remains unaddressed by Stenger.

Stenger argues, in contrast to Penrose, that the universe started out with maximal entropy (that is, maximal disorder) for an object of its size because it started as a black hole, and that the entropy then was much lower than now. Collins shows clearly that this is seriously mistaken. If the universe began as a black hole it would, on the contrary, have had far, far higher entropy then than it does now, contradicting the second law of thermodynamics. This is simply the result of standard calculations of entropy. Furthermore, Penrose shows that the end state of a collapsing universe would indeed have maximal entropy. It is an important part of Penrose's argument that the beginning and end states are completely asymmetric, with the end state vastly more like a "random" chaotic state and the beginning state ultra-special as described in the previous chapter. If the initial state were chosen at random, then it would be much more like the end state a collapsing universe reaches, i.e. utterly chaotic with no chance that any complex structures at all could develop.

Stenger also questions the fine-tuning of the "Hoyle resonance" described earlier. Yet, as Barnes notes, the most recent studies show this fine-tuning to be robust – especially taking into account the requirement that stars produce both carbon *and* oxygen, not carbon *or* oxygen. Thus Oberhummer *et al.*[12] show that, with a change of 0.4 per cent in the strength of the strong force, "carbon-based life appears to be impossible, since all the stars then would produce either almost solely carbon or oxygen, but could not produce both elements."

Another criticism Stenger makes is that theological conclusions are drawn from varying only one parameter at a time and keeping all the rest the same. He argues that a change in one parameter can be compensated for by a change in another.[13] If we vary just one parameter, there is a range of values within which the parameter must lie in order for the universe to be conducive to life, and, usually, a much bigger range in which it could conceivably lie (that's what we mean by saying the parameter is fine-tuned). A very good example is the strength of gravity as described above and in Chapter 5. To permit the development of intelligent life, the strength of gravity can be up to 3,000 times the value it takes in our universe; the range of possible values is between 0 and 10^{40} times the value in our universe. The probability that it is in the life-permitting range is then obtained by dividing 3,000 by 10^{40}, with the result 3×10^{-37} which we obtained in the last chapter.

If we vary two parameters at once, then we may indeed, as Stenger suggests, be able to extend the life-permitting range of each by varying these parameters together. Naïvely we could keep them in proportion so that we are still in the life-permitting region if both are doubled or trebled (though that won't work if some other relationship between parameters is required for life). We could certainly take the parameters out of their individual life-permitting ranges this way. However, as Barnes shows, the effect in this toy-like model is the opposite from that claimed by Stenger. This is because, not only has the range of values of the pair of parameters which are conducive to life been extended, but the set of possible pairs of values is also vastly extended compared to the possible range of a single parameter. The upshot is that when we take two parameters together we get an even smaller probability of being in the life-permitting range than when we take only one value at a time.

In reality, things are much worse for Stenger's argument than this naïve model would suggest. The problem is, as Barnes shows, that in reality there are many constraints to be satisfied for the universe to give rise to life, and the set of values of the parameters for which all are satisfied is in fact tiny in proportion to the possible set of values. He cites a paper by Barr and Khan as showing such a tiny life-permitting set of values when the masses of the up and down quarks are varied (these are fundamental particles – the proton comprises two up quarks and one down quark).[14] This is because the life-permitting pair of values has to satisfy nine independent constraints. These are essentially to do with the stability of atoms, and the existence of the right combinations of protons and neutrons, so that nuclear reactions can form the higher elements.

Max Tegmark and colleagues give other examples, for example relating the magnitude of the density perturbations to the cosmological constant, and the ratio of the number of matter particles to photons.[15] In an older paper, Tegmark noted that all of chemistry depends on two free parameters: the strength of the electromagnetic force and the ratio of electron and proton masses, and that "many seemingly vital processes hinge on a large number of 'coincidences'".[16] Tegmark states: "... it might thus appear as though there is a solution to an overdetermined problem with more equations (inequalities) than unknowns." If this is correct, and it seems highly likely, what it means is that we are indeed extremely fortunate that there exists *any* combination of parameters consistent with life. How come the many constraints on the values the parameters must take are compatible with each other so as to permit life at all? This is an extremely serious, indeed devastating, problem which atheists such as Stenger need to face up to.

Atheist strategy (2)

Coming to strategy (2), the multiverse hypothesis says that the universe certainly can be different, and indeed different universes actually exist. And it could be the case that the more universes you have the more chance there is of getting one with life. But there is a pretty big puzzle here too: namely, "Why does this particular multiverse exist as opposed to another?" It is often assumed that the multiverse in question is one with the same physical laws as ours but in which the constants which go into those laws vary. But if we abandon the idea that the constants are necessary given our set of physical laws, why should we not also abandon the idea that our set of laws is the only possible one?

Surely, in Hawking's terminology, there is a choice of equations into which fire somehow gets breathed and which give rise to universes. For each set of laws there is a further choice about how many universes are brought into existence, dependent on the number of permutations of the constants and on how many times each permutation is instantiated. That choice presumably leads to some universes in some multiverses having life (if, for a given set of laws, there are sets of constants which permit this), but the question is: what determines these various choices?

One notable cosmologist, Max Tegmark, mentioned above, has proposed in answer to this that all possible mathematical structures have physical existence.[17] That would certainly guarantee our universe's existence. But it takes us way beyond what physics can tell us, and most mathematicians and physicists think the idea is incoherent. You soon run into problems and paradoxes when you actually start to try and write down "all possible mathematical structures".[18] Certainly there seem to be conflicts in what actually exists as opposed to what can possibly exist. For example, *I* cannot simultaneously be sitting in my study writing about cosmic fine-tuning *and* be enjoying an exotic holiday trekking in the Peruvian Andes. Some copy of me in another universe could conceivably have taken a different course, but *I* could not simultaneously do both.

We have already begun to see that a multiverse still leaves the basic question open. It is simply modified to "Why this multiverse in which some universes have the right laws and sets of constants for life?" rather than "Why this universe which has the right laws and constants for life?" However, I do think that a multiverse can go some way towards explaining the fine-tuning. If we were to say that a multiverse with the same laws of nature as our universe exists but with all possible variations of constants instantiated in different universes, then that would ensure the existence of our own universe with its particular set of constants.

Some philosophers deny that this would make our existence any more likely than a single universe would.[19] They argue as follows. Label a particular universe within the multiverse "our universe". This universe would have the same, very low probability of being conducive to life as any other. In a long sequence of tosses of a coin ten heads will very occasionally occur consecutively. But if I come into a room and my friend tosses a coin ten times and gets ten heads, I should not immediately conclude he has been in there tossing coins for a very long time. The existence of many previous tosses makes no difference to the outcome for this particular set of tosses. Likewise, so the argument goes, the existence of many other universes does not make any difference to the probability that our universe will be conducive to life.

This is where I see a disanalogy between the multiverse and multiple firing squads. The existence of many other firing squads does not make any difference to *my* fate, just as many previous coin tosses does not affect the outcome of the present ten tosses. However, I can only come into existence if the constants of physics are just right. Perhaps a better analogy is this. My existence – indeed the existence of life at all – depends on a sharpshooter hitting a very small target from a very great distance, and that is highly improbable. If, however, there are many sharpshooters aiming at many small targets, that raises the probability that at least one of them will hit a target. Similarly, a multiverse in which the constants vary over all possible values gives a much better chance of life existing, and of me existing, than a random selection among universes. The mistake is to pick a random universe, call it "our universe", and then randomly pick the physical constants for it; the correct approach is randomly to assign physical constants to universes, and then to say that only one of the small number with the constants "just right" can become our universe.[20]

Having agreed, then, that multiverses can go some way towards explaining the fine-tuning of ours, we shall now have to delve a bit deeper into comparing this possible explanation with that of the divine design of our universe. Then we shall see that not only is the "basic question" still there, just rephrased as "Why this multiverse as opposed to another multiverse?", but there are many other problems besides. We begin our further exploration in the next chapter with a look at how in recent decades cosmologists have oscillated between single universe and multiverse models.

7

OF THE MAKING OF MANY UNIVERSES THERE IS NO END

Do there exist many worlds, or is there but a single world?
This is one of the most noble and exalted questions in the
study of Nature.

St Albertus Magnus (c. AD 1260)[1]

Universe or Multiverse? A Brief History of Recent Cosmology

In the search for the "ultimate theory of physics" physicists and cosmologists are driven by two considerations. The first is the specialness of the way the Big Bang and the laws of nature seem to be set up so that life can come into existence in the universe, as we discussed in Chapter 5. The second is the need in any case for a more fundamental theory to describe the physics at the earliest epochs in the universe's history and, purely from the point of view of physics, to combine the four fundamental forces into one. It is interesting to trace how over the last half century or so cosmologists have oscillated between single universe and multiverse theories. In the terminology of the last chapter, they can be said to have alternated between strategies (1) and (2), though not always with atheistic motives.

Chaotic cosmology

We begin this brief survey back in the late 1960s when the cosmologist Charles Misner came up with the "chaotic cosmology" programme, which sought to show that the initial conditions at the Big Bang didn't matter.[2] More or less any initial conditions would lead to a smooth universe such as we observe today. This is what Ernan McMullin dubbed "the *indifference principle*" in cosmology.[3] However, this idea was demolished by Stephen Hawking and a colleague of his, Barry Collins, in a paper written in 1973.[4] In order to give rise to life the universe must quickly approach a state in which it looks the same in all directions (technically it is "isotropic"). If that is not the case, then large-scale irregularities will make it impossible for galaxies and stars to form. Collins and Hawking showed that the probability of a universe like ours emerging from the Big Bang – looking the same in all directions in the sky to a high degree of accuracy – is actually zero.[5] You cannot have greater precision in the way the universe is set up than that.

Collins and Hawking turned to a multiverse (strategy (2)) to solve that problem. There are several ways of conceiving a multiverse. The simplest, and the one on which I shall concentrate, is as an infinite space in which there are enormously large regions, each region having its own set of parameters, although, as we shall see, there are several ways in which this version alone may be realized.

Oscillating universes

A second way of getting a multiverse is through successive expansions and contractions of a single universe, an idea associated with the physicist John Wheeler.[6] Wheeler speculated that the constants of nature and initial conditions might be randomly reselected at each "bounce", thus ensuring that at least one bounce gave the right conditions for life.

Wheeler's idea is fraught with problems. To begin with it relies on the universe being finite and positively curved so that recollapse occurs. But much more significant is the effect of the second law of thermodynamics, which tells us that the universe goes from a state of high order to one of increasing disorder. As we saw in Chapter 5, this universe started out highly ordered. Penrose points out that if the universe ends as a Big Crunch then that would be highly disordered. Thus the next bounce would start from high disorder, and it would be impossible for life to develop (that is, the probability of an ordered universe is not the same for each bounce – far from it, and after infinitely many bounces it would be zero). The upshot is that our particular bounce would be unique and the number of cycles in which life could occur would be very severely limited, thereby defeating the object of having infinitely many bounces in the first place! Indeed, according to Vilenkin's theorems, which we first met in Chapter 3, there could not in any case have been infinitely many bounces before ours.

The many worlds interpretation of quantum theory

A third way of getting a multiverse arises if one adopts a policy of realism with respect to all the possible outcomes of chance events in quantum theory. As we have seen, according to quantum theory a system is in a superposition or combination of states until a measurement is made. Then it "collapses" into a single state. Which state it collapses to is a matter of probability and is undetermined until the measurement is made. If you struggle with these ideas, you can take comfort from the great Nobel physics laureate Richard Feynman's remark, "I think I can safely say that nobody understands quantum mechanics"!

Hugh Everett III came up with an alternative interpretation of quantum theory according to which, when a measurement is made, the universe splits into many separate universes, each corresponding to one of the possible outcomes of the measurement. In order to solve the fine-tuning problem one would have to add to Everett's scheme the further hypothesis that the parameters take on different values in the branching universes and indeed a sufficient range of alternative values.[7]

There is a problem with invoking a multiverse to solve the problem identified by Collins and Hawking, which we should briefly consider before moving on to some of the latest theories. It is not the obvious one that a probability of zero means that the present universe cannot arise from the Big Bang. The probability of sticking a pin at random on the number line between 0 and 1 and it landing exactly on ½ is zero, but the number ½ certainly exists! However, with infinitely many tries the expected number of times the pin would land exactly on ½ is infinity times zero, which is mathematically undefined and therefore has no meaning. Likewise, even the existence of infinitely many universes does not guarantee that any are conducive to life. Our isotropic universe arose from the Big Bang, but taking infinitely many sets of randomly chosen starting conditions does not make it likely that it would do so. The extreme specialness of the starting conditions remains a problem for any atheist view of the matter.

Inflation

At the beginning of the 1980s Alan Guth proposed a way to solve some of the problems with the standard Big Bang, which he called the theory of "inflation".[8] Inflation is now widely accepted among cosmologists and seems to be supported by the latest satellite data. The theory postulates that the universe underwent an incredibly rapid period of accelerating expansion – called inflation – from 10^{-35} to 10^{-32} seconds after the origin. In that tiny fraction of a second the universe expanded from being 10^{-25} cm to 10 metres across. At that point, the much slower deceleration of the classical Big Bang took over. Such a rapid period of accelerating expansion, even if that short, would drive the density of the universe to the critical value and smooth out the differences between different parts of the universe, thus solving the problem to do with the universe looking the same in all directions. The claim is that a universe like ours would then virtually automatically come out of the Big Bang, or at the least is very much more likely to do so.

That sounds wonderful, but there were some serious problems with inflation. One serious problem from our point of view is that inflation itself needed fine-tuning; that is, parameters needed to be chosen specially! That is not very satisfactory for a theory that was meant to solve the problem of the need for fine-tuning. It is, however, symptomatic of a general trend: that fine-tuning just gets shifted up a level from the standard Big Bang into the more fundamental theory supposed to apply at the earliest times. The upshot in the case of inflation is that there has been an enormous inflation in the number of inflation theories. Writing in 2003, in a volume commemorating Stephen Hawking's sixtieth birthday, Paul Shellard listed 111 inflationary models, noting, I suspect with tongue in cheek, that "The most difficult model to rule out may well be supernatural inflation"![9]

The inflation era is also the "grand unified theory" era when three of the fundamental forces of nature are supposedly united; that is, the strong and weak nuclear forces and the electromagnetic force are united. Only gravity is not united with the other forces. At the end of the inflationary period this grand unified force splits into two, the strong and electro-weak forces. The forces split again at about 10^{-10} seconds after the origin with the electro-weak force splitting into separate electromagnetic and weak nuclear forces. That is about the time when we actually start to be confident about the physics. We can do experiments in the laboratory and the standard model of particle physics applies. The Large Hadron Collider at CERN in Geneva can reproduce the energies pertaining at this time, and somewhat earlier, though not anything like the energies pertaining at 10^{-32} seconds from the origin.

But back to inflation. The next step was to propose that inflation occurs in some places and not others and at different rates in the different parts of the universe where it does occur. The parts where inflation does occur would ultimately swamp the small non-inflating regions. Again this is a turn to strategy (2), as described in Chapter 6, namely a multiverse with different regions having different parameters. This picture was proposed by a Russian cosmologist now working at the University of Stanford, California, Andrei Linde. His idea is known as "chaotic inflation". Another variant is "eternal inflation" in which infinitely many different bubble universes are formed by inflation, with bubbles forming within bubbles ad infinitum.

String theory and M-theory

We are still not quite at the theory of everything (TOE). That is the theory which is said to apply to the very first 10^{-43} seconds from the origin. During that time one needs a theory that combines all the forces of nature. That is to say, it combines Einstein's general theory of relativity, which is the theory of gravity, with quantum mechanics, which applies to the other forces and describes the very small.

We do not know what that theory is, but the leading contender is string theory, one of whose main pioneers has been Leonard Susskind. String theory postulates that the ultimate building blocks of matter are not point-like particles but tiny, one-dimensional objects called strings. By tiny I mean really tiny: some 10^{-33} cm across.

String theory aims to solve some of the problems with the standard model of particle physics, especially the existence of infinite quantities like mass and charge. According to string theory, the elementary particles we observe are actually different modes of vibration of the strings. An important complication is that these vibrations occur in more than the three dimensions of space that we are used to; indeed the theory is only consistent if there are as many as ten space–time dimensions. M-theory, the overarching generalization of string theory favoured by Stephen Hawking and others, unifies what were originally five different versions of the theory, and in it there are eleven space–time dimensions. The reason we only see three extended dimensions is that these other dimensions get curled up very small. Quite why this is so remains something of a mystery, although, as noted in

Chapter 5, the extra dimensions would have to be curled up very small for the universe to be compatible with life.

The original aim of string theory was to calculate particle masses; that is to say, strategy (1), in the nomenclature of Chapter 6, was pursued. The theory has always been dogged by its lack of connection with observation and experiment, so the main motivation has been that it is beautifully mathematically elegant (though see later) and solves some theoretical problems. It is still the aim of some string theorists to calculate everything and some believe that is possible in principle, though some parameters (like the cosmological constant) still seem to need strategy (2). Nevertheless, nothing has been calculated in practice, so some string theorists, notably Leonard Susskind, have taken the turn to strategy (2) anyway.

I had the privilege of being invited to a symposium in Stanford, where Susskind and Linde work, in 2005, to discuss multiverses and the latest ideas in string theory. Over a convivial dinner on the first evening, Susskind turned to me and said that he had a book coming out with the title *The Cosmic Landscape: String Theory and the Illusion of Intelligent Design*.[10] Susskind may not be aware of the important distinction between Intelligent Design, the flawed idea of seeing God as filling gaps in the processes of biological evolution, and the more general and robust design argument based on the question as to why laws of nature take the particular form they do. But be that as it may, Susskind went on to tell me that his book, now published, would close by saying, "If there is a God, she has taken great pains to make herself irrelevant." Indeed, this is the provocative penultimate sentence of the book, and our discussion that first evening foreshadowed an interesting and lively few days at the symposium!

Susskind and his colleagues now talk about the "landscape of string theory", an idea inaugurated in a much-cited paper by Shamit Kachru, Renate Kallosh, Andrei Linde, and Sandip Trivedi (and abbreviated KKLT).[11] They find that there is not just one but many solutions of the theory, anything from 10^{100} to 10^{500} or possibly even 10^{1000} solutions. The further claim is that a universe can "tunnel" between solutions. The solutions are stable for billions of years; then another universe pops up as a region moves to another solution of the equations. This feeds in very neatly to the eternal inflation idea. If it works, and it is a big if, eternal inflation would be the means whereby the string theory landscape is populated. It is also true that if there is a theory that in some sense naturally gives rise to many universes, then that gives plausibility to the idea of a multiverse. However, as I shall explain in the next chapter, there are many problems with such an approach.

Conformal cyclic cosmology

Roger Penrose has come up with another proposal called conformal cyclic cosmology. Basically Penrose sees the end result of the vast expansion of the universe as providing the seed for another Big Bang.[12] This is because, if all the matter in the universe just decays into radiation, the sense of time is lost: photons get from A to B instantaneously. Penrose thinks that is like the Big Bang and by some subtle mathematics that the universe can be rescaled (that is the meaning of "conformal" in this context) so that the infinitely large becomes infinitely small and it all starts over again.

Penrose doesn't think inflation solves the problem that the universe had to start out highly ordered, a view which now seems to be endorsed by one of the theory's pioneers, Paul Steinhardt.[13] It turns out that inflation is itself highly improbable. A flat universe, as is needed for life, is vastly more likely to arise if there is no inflation, but is highly unlikely in either case. Steinhardt also criticizes eternal inflation for being unable to make predictions about the probability of fine-tuning because, if there are infinitely many regions of different kinds inflating at different rates or not inflating at all, probability calculations are rendered impossible. However,

Penrose recognizes that black holes evaporate and remove information and thus entropy (disorder) from the universe, ideas associated with Hawking in fact, though Hawking has changed his mind about information loss. Thus for Penrose the end of the universe is now like its beginning.

It should be noted that this model applies to an infinite open universe in which all black holes have time to evaporate. It is quite unlike the more conventional closed cyclic models (the oscillating models discussed above) where, as Penrose shows, the beginning and end are totally asymmetric, with an ordered beginning and a highly disordered end. Indeed, Penrose also shows that matters are much worse for the more conventional open infinite universe than they are for the closed model with a "Big Crunch". That is because the probability of selecting an ordered universe from all the possibilities decreases as the size of universe increases. Thus a vanishingly small fraction of open infinite universes possess the order and structure our universe does.[14]

In terms of the fine-tuning, there may be some room in the conformal cyclic model for varying parameters in successive "cycles", though this is not spelled out. However, it seems to me that the uniqueness of the physical laws and the fact that they give rise to a universe like ours at all still requires explanation. If the universe has a highly ordered beginning, which is repeated at each cycle, the question does not go away but is simply rephrased: why does the universe possess that property?

It has to be said that Penrose's theory is highly contentious among cosmologists, and his earlier statements about the asymmetry between the beginning and end of the universe are much more robust scientifically. Even Penrose himself is aware that many details of the conformal cyclic model remain to be filled in. Moreover, observations which Penrose argues support his model are disputed, as is the theory itself. One point counting against it is that for the rescaling to work all particles have to lose their mass, whereas, as far as we know, the electron mass is stable.

The ekpyrotic universe

There are a number of other cosmological proposals on the table for how our universe began. One, the ekpyrotic universe of Neil Turok and Paul Steinhardt, would see the universe we inhabit as a three-dimensional surface of a four-dimensional space.[15] Two such surfaces, called branes, collide, and that is what starts off the Big Bang. In this way the model is supposed to avoid a singularity at the beginning and to give the universe a homogeneous and flat starting configuration, just as inflation was designed to do. However, as we noted in Chapter 3, the theorems of Vilenkin and his colleagues show that even these brane universes ultimately lead back to a singularity.

The proliferation of multiverse models has spawned multiple treatments in the popular scientific literature. For example, John Gribbin takes his readers on a dizzying tour of the possibilities, but exhibits considerable overconfidence both in the existence of multiverses, for which there is no evidence, and in their actually solving the fine-tuning problem.[16] As we shall see in the next chapter, even the latter claim is highly doubtful. Brian Greene describes nine variations on the multiverse idea, although, to give him credit, Greene acknowledges: "The subject of parallel universes is highly speculative."[17]

The great Russian physicist Lev Landau once made the perceptive remark that "cosmologists are often in error, but seldom in doubt." With the bewildering proliferation of models and lack of observational constraint, it seems there is a considerable degree of truth in this. However, Christians do not all reject the multiverse concept. On the contrary, there are a number who enthusiastically embrace the idea – which leads me to consider…

Why might Christians Welcome Multiverses?

Theologian Wolfhart Pannenberg believes that an infinite world remains "a marginal possibility for the Christian theology of creation", even though Cardinal Nicholas of Cusa thought it was especially befitting the perfection of the Creator.[18] Pannenberg would particularly object if it led to the necessity of the world rather than its contingency. Against infinite, steady-state, and oscillatory models, Pannenberg offers the challenge, "Should a theological interest in the finiteness and irreversible historicity of the world also become involved?"[19] It is bold in this day and age for a theologian to be reminding scientists of the fundamentals of their trade. In this case, Pannenberg is referring back to the theological idea that the universe is the free creation of God. It is contingent, meaning that it could be different from what it is. For Pannenberg, all possibilities are not embraced in an infinite cosmos, since that would lead us back in the direction of the world being necessary and would violate the way the biblical God acts historically through unique contingent events.[20]

While Georges Lemaître generally kept his science and theology in two compartments, he nevertheless always stuck to a finite-sized universe, apparently on theological grounds, namely that a finite universe is comprehensible to humans made in the image of God in a way an infinite universe would not be. I confess to being closer to Pannenberg and Lemaître on this issue, as will become clear, but let me briefly look at four Christians who believe in, or are happy to accept, both God and a multiverse. One is a scientist–theologian, the second a philosopher, the third a cosmologist, and the fourth a theologian who trained as a philosopher.

The scientist–theologian Arthur Peacocke

The late Arthur Peacocke was a scientist and theologian, the only person in a hundred years to obtain higher doctorates in both science and theology from the University of Oxford. He was among the pioneers of the modern dialogue between science and religion, and he favoured a multiverse. What counts for Peacocke is the potentiality of the whole ensemble of universes, rather than one universe in particular, to produce cognizing subjects.[21] The fine-tuning argument still applies, given that the multiverse of which our universe is a member has the right parameters for persons to evolve somewhere in it, in our particular universe at the very least of course.

Peacocke and others would be unruffled, as indeed am I, by the analogous seeming waste in biological evolution, with its dead ends and multiple extinctions, seeing this rather as God's mechanism for producing intelligent life. Indeed, for Peacocke, God creates through the interplay of law and chance, with chance being the mechanism whereby creation explores the space of potentialities and ultimately evolves intelligent life. It is just that the space of potentialities is now far vaster, indeed infinite. On any account, universe or multiverse, the emergence of persons is truly astonishing and unpredictable a priori. Perhaps God's handiwork could be seen as even more glorious on the multiverse view.

The philosopher Robin Collins

Robin Collins is a philosopher who certainly thinks that the fine-tuning is real and in need of explanation, and in an essay in 2003 seemed to treat the design and multiverse hypotheses as alternatives, admittedly without much discussion of the multiverse hypothesis.[22] But in the more recent volume on multiverses, edited by Bernard Carr,[23] he takes a similar view to Peacocke.

On the theistic hypothesis, says Collins, the creation would reflect God's infinitely creative capacities, so physical reality might be much larger than a single universe. The idea would be that God expresses his infinite creativity, rather than that he simply and purposively creates a single universe with life in it. That was the view of Nicholas of Cusa and of Giordano Bruno. Collins thinks that the idea is supported today by inflationary multiverse models and the fact that cosmology has shown us a progressively larger visible part of the universe. He also thinks that creating a multiverse through a single physical universe-generating mechanism, as seems to be on offer with inflation, maybe as combined with the landscape of string theory idea, would be a befittingly elegant way for God to do this. Moreover, if there is a multiverse generator, then *it* needs design, just as a single universe needed to be designed if it were to give rise to life. The fine-tuning problem is merely shifted from the universe to the multiverse.

Collins argues that very specific laws must be in place for the multiverse generator to produce a life-conducive member universe. The fine-tuning of the constants themselves, however, is weakened, provided that the generator produces sufficient variation. The production of enough variation has always seemed a somewhat hidden assumption in the past, and a problem for many universe-generating mechanisms, but Collins thinks M-theory might do the trick.

Another argument that Collins brings to bear is that the laws of nature are mathematically beautiful and elegant. That seems to me to be true, and is almost a commonplace in physics, but it might be undermined if the landscape of string theory really existed. Susskind himself calls this a Rube Goldberg machine, which is "American English" for what in "British English" we call a Heath Robinson.[24]

More recently Collins has argued that the multiverse doesn't solve the fine-tuning problem.[25] This is essentially because, if we were in a multiverse, we ought to be typical observers within it, whereas in fact we are highly atypical of the kinds of observers a multiverse would produce. We return to this argument in the next chapter – indeed to several forms of it.

The cosmologist Don Page

Don Page is a cosmologist who is both an evangelical Christian and a multiverse proponent. Like Bernard Carr, Page has been one of Stephen Hawking's collaborators over many years. Page favours the Everett version of the multiverse in which a new universe arises corresponding to every possible outcome of a quantum measurement.[26] But he also argues that God might prefer an elegant theory, such as string/M-theory without free parameters, that would lead to a multiverse, but with the deliberate intention that there be life somewhere within it. He says, like Collins, that the beauty and elegance of that theory might be an argument for its design by God, though the argument from the design of the constants would be undercut. Susskind would seem to disagree about elegance, which is strange since the aesthetic appeal of a theory has been a driving force in physics, and notable exemplars would include Einstein and Paul Dirac.

The theologian Keith Ward

A theologian who does not object to multiverses in principle is Keith Ward, who is Emeritus Regius Professor of Divinity at Oxford. The problem would be the goodness of the universes created, since the God Christians believe in would only create universes which were overall better to exist than not.[27] They could not therefore contain overwhelming unmitigated evil. However, with the models we are presented with in cosmology, there is no selection of which universes exist on such a moral basis, so Ward's problem is a real one.

In summary, it is certainly the case that some Christians believe in multiverses, and there is no doubt that Christian theology could adapt to the existence of other universes as it has to many other scientific discoveries, However, it seems to me that there are many problems with the multiverses on offer in modern cosmology. I address these problems in the next chapter.

8

MULTIPLE PROBLEMS FOR MULTIVERSES

Father Pirrone thought what a mess the world must seem to one who knew neither mathematics nor theology. "Oh, Lord, only Thy omniscience could have devised so many complications."

Giuseppe di Lampedusa[1]

Introduction
The whole idea of multiverses, including the latest string landscape idea, is fraught with problems, both scientific and philosophical, and I shall now go on to examine them under nine subheadings.[2]

1. Speculative Physics
It is important to recognize that the physics associated with multiverses is speculative, to say the least, especially when it comes to string theory. Some eminent physicists are sceptical about string theory per se. Richard Feynman some long time ago objected that string theorists were not calculating anything,[3] yet to calculate is still the aim for at least some members of the string theory community. For example, Kane *et al.* think that the particle masses are calculable in principle.[4] However, these authors acknowledge that the cosmological constant may require

the anthropic approach, which they interpret in terms of a multiverse. Thus, they arrive at a strange mix of strategies (1) and (2) in the terminology I introduced in Chapter 6; that is, both a more fundamental theory that calculates most of the parameters *and* a multiverse.

On the other hand, the continued lack of calculation has prompted a couple of books to come out which are sceptical of the whole string/M-theory enterprise. One, *Not Even Wrong* by Peter Woit,[5] takes its title from the habit of the famous physicist Wolfgang Pauli of sitting at the back of a research seminar, and, at the end, challenging the quaking PhD student with the words "That's wrong." Apparently one time Pauli thought that an article by a young theoretical physicist was so bad that he said instead, "That's not even wrong", meaning it was hardly worthy of consideration. The second significant book challenging string theory is by Lee Smolin and is entitled *The Trouble with Physics*.[6]

Even the string theory community is divided over whether the landscape, the multiverse version of the theory, exists.[7] Some think the solutions are really different theories and therefore to talk about tunnelling from one to another is quite wrong.

The trouble with postulating the existence of universes other than our own is that they cannot even in principle be observed. That is a very important difference from the many planets comparison that is sometimes made. Given billions of planets there is bound to be one like ours the right distance from its parent star, and so on, for life to arise. Well, we can observe other planets; we have detected planets outside the solar system, and, having originally detected large Jupiter-like planets, we are now starting to detect planets that are more like the earth. There is nothing strange or startling about that. But other universes? Well, they cause no effect whatever in our own universe because no signal from them can ever reach us.

I must say I find it rather intriguing that there is almost a "law" at work here too. As theories progress towards "ultimacy", as we get closer and closer to the final theory of everything (TOE), so the observational and experimental support diminishes to nothing. We are, after all, talking about regimes where the energies exceed what is attainable in the laboratory, in particle accelerators, by factors of billions. It is almost as if God is having a bit of fun at our expense, putting the ultimate just beyond our grasp; or maybe, through its straining at the very limits, physics is pointing beyond itself to its transcendent source.

History might also caution us regarding TOEs, since we thought we were here before. At the end of the nineteenth century some physicists thought physics was all tied up bar some loose ends, which were to determine the constants experimentally to ever more decimal places. They could not have been more wrong! And might it not just be, again, that there are further depths of nature yet to be uncovered which point to the unlimited creativity of the Creator? Who is to say that there might not be further fundamental levels of explanation beyond string/M-theory (if that itself is correct) that are even more inaccessible? This is not to put any constraints on the quest for such theories. I am all in favour of pursuing the science as far as it can go, even if in this case it is not clear whether it is physics or metaphysics that is being pursued. No, it is just to urge a word of caution when faced with over-optimistic claims to have reached the final theory.

Martin Rees (Lord Rees of Ludlow) is one of Britain's most distinguished cosmologists. In one of his books he describes himself as a "cautious empiricist" who starts to feel at home when familiar physics can be applied to the universe, which he says is the first thousandth of a second from the origin and later.[8] He is rightly uneasy about how cosmology is popularized:

> First, if we claim too often to be stripping the last veil from the face of God, or making discoveries that overthrow all previous ideas, we will surely erode our credibility. It would be prudent, as well as seemly, to rein in the hyperbole a bit. Second, one should not

conflate things that are well established with those that
are not yet in that state.[9]

On the other hand, in another book Rees expresses his preference
for a multiverse over design, even though he describes the
multiverse idea as "highly speculative" and his preference "no
more than a hunch".[10] The physics that would yield the most
popular versions of the multiverse applies not to one thousandth
of a second after the origin, but the first 10^{-32} seconds or even
the first 10^{-43} seconds. It is a quite interesting example of another
ideologically driven rather than evidence-based preference. Even
though Rees recognizes that science is powerless to answer the
question of why there is anything at all, he still goes in the
direction Dietrich Bonhoeffer indicated in seeing a multiverse as
removing the need for God as an explanation.

Leonard Susskind, one of the founders of string theory,
likewise sees no need for God if his string landscape version of the
multiverse is correct. He writes: "The laws of gravity, quantum
mechanics, and a rich Landscape together with the laws of large
numbers are all that's needed to explain the friendliness of our
patch of the universe." Susskind, like the early Hawking, Rees,
and Sciama, acknowledges: "The ultimate existential question,
'Why is there Something rather than Nothing?' has no more
or less of an answer than before anyone ever heard of String
Theory."[11] Nevertheless, as we saw earlier, Susskind ends his book
by stating this: "If there is a God, she [*sic*] has taken great pains
to make herself redundant."[12]

2. Paradoxes of Infinity

Multiverse models generally assume that there are an infinite
number of universes. This is true of the landscape of string theory
too, since even if there are a finite number of solutions (say 10^{500})
these would be reproduced infinitely many times.

There is a problem about the existence of actual infinities
in nature. Mathematicians happily talk about and manipulate

different degrees of infinity, but there are many paradoxes when you think about infinite numbers of things existing in the real world. For example, consider the hotel with infinitely many rooms conceived by the great German mathematician David Hilbert. All the rooms in Hilbert's Hotel are full. Even so, one can very easily make room for infinitely many more guests! All one has to do is tell the person in Room 1 to move to Room 2, the one in Room 2 to go to Room 4, the one in Room 3 to go to Room 6, and so on. Then all the even numbered rooms are full, but the odd numbered ones are all free! So, Hilbert's Hotel has room for infinitely many new guests. An infinite library would function similarly. Even if every shelf were full, there would always be room for more books, because there would be infinitely many shelves and one could shift existing books just as one moved the guests in Hilbert's Hotel. An author who has insightfully explored the notion of an infinite library, and other such paradoxes, is the Argentine magic realist writer Jorge Luis Borges.[13]

The above paradoxes concern the simultaneous existence of infinitely many things. But there are also paradoxes that relate to the possibility of an infinite past during which there are infinitely many events. These paradoxes add weight to the claims of William Lane Craig and others that the universe must be finite in time as well as space.

Consider the following counting paradox. Alice has been counting from infinite time past and is coming to an end today: … -3, -2, -1, 0. But why does she end now? Why did she not finish yesterday, or the day before, or indeed at any particular point in the past? Arguably she should have ended long ago given that she has been counting from minus infinity.

In fact, as pointed out by John Taylor,[14] there is no real contradiction here; Alice could have finished any day in the past, but just happened to finish today. However, a contradiction can be introduced by also including the principle of sufficient reason as a premise to the argument – that is, by asserting that if there is no sufficient reason why a process ends at one time rather than another, then it cannot end at either time. Taylor further argues that, while the principle of sufficient reason is not a necessary truth, a theory that gives a reason is to be metaphysically preferred to one that does not. A theory that allowed an actual infinity would leave unanswerable the question, "Why did Alice stop counting today rather than yesterday or any other day?" In the multiverse context, the question "Why do we exist here and now when we could have existed in infinitely many alternative space–time locations?" is equally unanswerable. And, still in the context of a universe with an infinite past, there is the problem raised by the second law of thermodynamics, which essentially says that the universe is running down and will eventually end up cold and dead: why is it not already cold and dead if it has been dying for an infinite time past?

One of the earliest and simplest versions of the multiverse was considered as long ago as 1979 by George Ellis and Geoff Brundrit.[15] This kind of multiverse was simply an open, infinite, single universe of the standard FLRW (Friedmann–Lemaître–Robertson–Walker) kind discussed in Chapter 1 with density fluctuations superimposed (a "pure" FLRW universe, being perfectly homogeneous and isotropic, would have no galaxies and stars). The problem these authors identified is that in such an infinite universe there will be infinitely many identical copies of me writing a book on the Big Bang and its relationship with theology. This follows from there being infinitely many galaxies but only a finite number of configurations of the DNA molecule.

There will also be copies of me who differ very slightly. Some of them will be writing about multiverses, while others will decide to put their feet up and watch TV instead! Of course the same phenomenon of infinite replication will occur in other more recently proposed versions of the multiverse, such as eternal inflation, in which parameters vary across universes. It is quite bizarre even to begin to think about this. Some philosophers and mathematicians think that the existence of infinitely many universes is ruled out because of the paradoxes. Indeed George Ellis and colleagues have revisited this issue more recently.[16] They raise the issue of the "non-constructability" of actual infinities – an infinity can always be added to (as with Hilbert's Hotel) and can never be completed. They also raise some of the irresolvable paradoxes in set theory, such as Russell's paradox, which is even stronger than the ones we raised above. The great philosopher Bertrand Russell famously asked us to consider the set of all sets that are not members of themselves. The question, "Is this set a member of itself?" leads to a logical contradiction. If it is it isn't, and if it isn't it is!

I do not quite see the paradoxes of infinite sets as logically precluding their physical existence, but a theory without paradoxes and with fewer unanswerable questions is surely to be preferred.

3. The Criterion of Simplicity

The existence of a vast ensemble of universes is not a simple hypothesis. Scientists normally opt for the simplest of competing hypotheses that explain the phenomena under consideration, and there is no reason not to adopt the same criterion when it comes to metaphysical hypotheses. The multiverse hypothesis does not seem to be simple at all (we defer until Chapter 10 discussion of whether the theistic hypothesis is simple). The principle of Ockham's razor tells us that we should not multiply entities needlessly: we should choose the most economical of competing hypotheses in terms of number of entities.

As noted in Chapter 6, a question one needs to ask is "Why this multiverse?" That applies to the "string landscape" idea as much as any of the others, and even to produce the landscape some choices within string theory have been made. That is to say, to choose the string landscape version of the multiverse is to make one choice among many possibilities; to choose a subset of possibilities within string theory for realization is to make another choice. As we saw in Chapter 6, we have to ask what determines these choices. And the very fact of having to ask these questions implies that the hypothesis is not simple.

It may be that this problem is ameliorated if there is a theory that we can accept on other grounds which naturally gives rise to a multiverse. The trouble with the multiverse theories on offer, including (perhaps especially) the string landscape version, is that we have no such grounds. We are back to the first problem discussed above, namely the lack of contact with experiment and observation and the speculative nature of the physics. In order to be convincing, the string theory community needs both to come to a consensus about the existence of the landscape in the first place, and also to provide some unequivocal predictions that can be verified. If nothing is predicted and everything explained anthropically (meaning on the basis of a multiverse), then I agree with those in the literature who argue that this is tantamount to giving up on physics.

I agree with philosopher Tim Mawson that in order for the multiverse hypothesis to guarantee that our fine-tuned universe exists, one needs to adopt something like Max Tegmark's "maximal multiverse" discussed briefly in Chapter 6.[17] As I pointed out there, this is problematic for several reasons (for example, not least that not all possible universes *can* exist, though for the sake of argument I ignore that in what follows). Mawson agrees that simplicity is an important criterion, but he also believes (against me) that Tegmark's version of the multiverse is simple. This is because you do not have to specify which universes or mathematical structures exist – they all do – and for Mawson it is simple because it only contains one "type" of entity, a universe; that it contains infinitely many "tokens" of this entity is not important for Mawson's evaluation of simplicity. However, Mawson believes that the multiverse still suffers from a serious, indeed devastating, drawback, as explained in the next section.

4. Multiverses and Predictability

The turn from strategy (1) (a theory of everything that calculates the physical constants) to strategy (2) (a multiverse in which the constants vary) implies a move away from predictability, which had been a cornerstone of the scientific method. This is not just predictability of physical parameters, but predictability in general based on the existence of order in the universe.

Suppose some unexplained phenomenon arises in the laboratory. Instead of trying to explain it rationally using science, the temptation is now to say, "We just happen to be in a universe which exhibits that phenomenon." After all, given the vast ensemble of universes, if something is possible it will happen somewhere sometime in some universe, or so it is said. Such theories are not falsifiable (though see section 6 below).

There are several similar arguments of this kind, and we shall describe one now and two more in sections 7 and 8. In Tegmark's maximal multiverse, which is of course the only version of the multiverse to guarantee the existence of this universe, would we not expect there to be far more disordered universes in the ensemble than ordered ones? And, in particular, would there not be universes which are sufficiently ordered to bring intelligent life into being, and then, at some random moment, degenerate into chaos? Mawson crystallizes this by saying that we rely on, and need, the future to resemble the past.[18] Indeed "morally sensitive and significantly free creatures" in general require this. The principle of induction is the assertion that nature does indeed work this way, enabling us to make reliable inferences, but it is not a necessary truth. It does not follow from the fact that it has worked up till now that it will work in the same way in the future, and indeed there are infinitely many ways in which it may cease to do so. So, in the maximal multiverse, there would be infinitely many creatures identical to ourselves up till now whose inductive procedures collapsed in the next few seconds. Thus, on the basis of the maximal multiverse, the probability that induction goes on working indefinitely is infinitesimally small, since the relatively small number of universes in which induction continues to work is completely swamped by the enormous number in which it fails to do so.

This is a devastating problem for Tegmark's maximal multiverse. On the other hand, whether or not God is a simpler explanation, the theistic hypothesis would render it unsurprising that significantly free creatures inhabited a universe conducive to their exercising that freedom in morally responsible ways, since God is likely to bring about a universe with that intention.

5. The Cosmological Constant

We saw in Chapter 5 that possibly the most outstanding problem in cosmology is the fine-tuning of the cosmological constant, Λ. This is the term originally introduced into his equations by Einstein, and set to a particular value to make the universe static. If he had put it to zero, he would have predicted the expansion and arrived at the Big Bang theory. Subsequently he and de Sitter did adopt a zero value and obtained a Big Bang type of model, while Lemaître retained a positive value in his alternative Big Bang model. Observations by Nobel prize-winning scientists Perlmutter, Schmidt, and Riess at the end of the 1990s indicated that Λ takes a very small but positive value. However, there is a problem, because the observed value of Λ is smaller by a factor of 10^{120} than the value obtained by quantum vacuum calculations. This is probably the biggest mismatch between theory and observation or experiment in the whole of science!

The answer cosmologists have come up with to this one? You've guessed it, and we have already touched upon it above. It is a multiverse. In fact, in the string theory landscape the different universes represent different values of Λ. If a universe starts with a very high value of Λ, it will "tunnel" billions upon billions of times until a universe eventually arises with the small value of Λ that our universe has. Steven Weinberg had previously argued that a multiverse is required to give a space–time region with Λ

very low as in our universe, and the string landscape provides a mechanism for producing such a region (universe).

This looks like a great success. However, several problems present themselves. First, it has not been shown that all the values of Λ are in fact worked through. Suppose we make the assumption (which may not be warranted) that Λ must lie between zero and the calculated value (which is 10^{120} times the observed value). It is then possible that the realization of a large but finite (greater than 10^{120}) number of solutions would make it likely that a value in the observed region would be realized. That seems to be the claim of string landscape proponents with figures from 10^{100} to 10^{500} being cited for the number of solutions.[19] However, one may question whether enough solutions are realized, or even if a finite number of solutions is adequate, if all other parameters (strengths of forces etc.) vary across the landscape. It has been noted that if the Planck mass (the mass at which quantum gravity effects become important) or the amplitude of the primordial density perturbations (discussed in Chapter 5) is varied as well as Λ, then the probability of getting a universe like ours may well be low (contrary to Stenger's argument about varying parameters simultaneously, as we saw in Chapter 6).[20] And if it were not low, one would still be able to ask, "Why not?" Why are sufficiently many solutions realized so as to make a universe like ours likely to come into existence? How is it that nature has contrived to make a universe compatible with life by this particular means?

The advance over the original eternal inflationary scheme is the provision of a mechanism at a more fundamental theoretical level for producing the multiverse. That is to say, the multiverse constitutes different solutions of string theory but these are brought into existence via the eternal inflationary scheme. However, the physics remains speculative and, as I mentioned above, it is disputed whether the landscape is established at all. For example, Tom Banks thinks it is wrong to regard the different solutions as states of the same theory.[21] Even if the landscape does exist there is still a choice of string theory variables to be made to realize it. The KKLT (Kachru, Kallosh, Linde, and Trivedi) paper, which I referred to in Chapter 7, considered only one of the five types of string theory, so that the old question, "Why this selection?", still arises. In addition, the calculations need to be much more detailed to be convincing (first of all, to the string theory community).

Even if this scheme worked there would still remain the question as to whether the value of Λ that pertains in our universe is typical of the range of values that would be life permitting. If there is a multiverse, it ought to be typical of the life-permitting values, since we ought to regard ourselves as typical observers, a point that will recur later. Our universe would be a random member of the subset of universes that give rise to life. The question then is, "Does it look like that or is it more special than that?"

Now calculations show that the average value of Λ that would be compatible with life is quite a bit more than the value we observe. If it is too large, galaxies cannot form in the early universe by gravitational collapse. However, the first calculations showed that it could be 100 times more than the observed value; that figure came down with subsequent calculations, but it still looks a bit too high. In other words, the actual value we observe looks a bit too low, a fact acknowledged by Steven Weinberg, who did the calculations, in the book on multiverses edited by Bernard Carr.[22] Paul Davies in that volume also thinks that Λ is not "minimally biophilic" – that is, not "just good enough" for life – as would be expected on the multiverse hypothesis. Davies thinks the value is rather too low for that – perhaps even "optimally biophilic"; that is, giving the value most compatible with life.[23] Thus we seem to be observing a value of Λ that is a bit too special, though not enormously so by astronomical standards.

Of course, even if we thought that Λ was explained on the basis of a multiverse (and I can agree that it is a parameter which comes closest to being explained), there could still be many other parameters of our universe besides Λ which are more highly tuned than is strictly required for our own existence. It looks as though there are and I shall return to this point in section 7, examining one of them in some detail.

6. Fine-Tuning Required for a Multiverse?

Some multiverse models require an element of fine-tuning for there to be a multiverse in the first place. An example is that the overall mean density must be less than or equal to the critical value so that the universe as a whole is "open" and infinite. Remember that the universe would be "closed" and finite in size were the density to be above the critical value.

It may well not be likely that the density is below the critical value, as is required for the universe to be infinite, given that in principle it could take any value from an enormously large range. A priori it might well be greater than the critical value, in which case the universe is not infinite, but finite. There are technical issues involved in translating the values the density can take into probability,[24] but the simplest and most obvious, albeit naïve, way to do this would make an infinite universe extremely unlikely.

It may be that the landscape and other multiverse theories are already faced with the possibility of observational falsification for this reason. Incidentally, although a single observer may pass through a finite number of solutions of string theory, Susskind tells us that "the global space contains an infinite number of such histories."[25]

Data on the cosmic background radiation from the WMAP satellite has been examined in detail. The very tiny fluctuations in the temperature of the radiation have been taken to confirm the predictions of inflation. But there is a small discrepancy, namely that the fluctuations are much weaker at the largest angular scales than would be expected on the standard flat, infinite universe model. Moreover, the best fit to the data for the density is marginally greater than the critical value. Some cosmologists, notably Jean-Pierre Luminet and colleagues, interpret this to mean that we are indeed living in a finite universe which is closing back in on itself.[26] The size of the universe limits large-scale fluctuations in a finite universe, according to Luminet, and such a universe has the bizarre property, arising naturally for positively curved space in Einstein's general relativity, that we can be looking at the same bit of sky in different directions. What this would be saying is that we could almost be seeing right round the universe and there simply would not be other regions "outside" ours. This is very tentative and controversial (the error of 2 per cent in density, for example, could still just bring the density to critical or below), but the model which is proposed here at least has the merit of contact with observation and openness to empirical enquiry – and would avoid all the paradoxes of infinity.

In fact, the more recent Planck satellite confirms weak temperature fluctuations at large angular scales, and other anomalies in the cosmic background radiation, but does not seem to support this particular model.[27] Suppose, then, that this particular finite model were indeed eliminated by observation. It would still be the case that we could never be sure that we really inhabited an infinite universe. John Barrow makes just this point.[28] In fact, either of two options is possible. We may think we are in an open, infinite universe when we just inhabit an under-dense part of a closed, finite universe, *or* we think we are in a closed, finite universe when we inhabit an over-dense part of an open, infinite universe. The one case that would be empirically verifiable would be that in which the universe is finite and sufficiently "small", as is the model of Luminet *et al.*, for us to be able to "see all round it". In practice, that means a universe whose space dimension is less than the distance to our horizon; that is, about 46 billion light years – still quite large by terrestrial standards!

The multiverse proponent might mitigate some of the problems we have listed so far by opting for a finite-sized but enormously large overarching space, instead of an infinite space. Of course, this finite space would have to be large enough to accommodate sufficient variation to ensure that our set of parameters is selected in some region. But, of course, many questions would still remain, not least, "Why is the overarching space as large as it is so that some region within it will be conducive to life?"

7. The Order of the Universe at the Beginning

Sir Roger Penrose, former Professor of Mathematics at Oxford and outstanding cosmologist, poses a massive problem to inflation and indeed all attempts to explain the specialness of the Big Bang on the basis of a multiverse. We looked at the first part of this story in Chapter 5 and will recap on this in a bit more detail before going on to the more devastating aspect.

As we saw in Chapter 5, Penrose is concerned with the amount of order there was at the beginning. Order can be measured (by a quantity called entropy) and it decreases over time (though entropy increases as order decreases). This is what the second law of thermodynamics tells us. I gave the example in Chapter 5 of knocking my coffee cup on the floor and seeing the coffee ooze into the carpet and cool down. Another example would be to put red and blue paint into a pot and give the pot a stir, though even without the stir the result will eventually be the same.[29] A hybrid purple colour will result and then no amount of stirring will get us back to the original separation of red and blue. The reason for this is that there are overwhelmingly more states of the system with the red and blue paint molecules mixed up than with them neatly separated, so the purple colour is much more probable than the red–blue split. Entropy is simply a measure of the probability of a particular configuration. In the case of the paint, a red–blue separation would be very low entropy compared with an overall purple-looking colour.

In Chapter 5 I described Penrose's calculation of the initial entropy of the universe. He says that only one out of something like $10^{10^{123}}$ possible universe configurations would have the order and structure which our universe does. That is the order necessary to produce a cosmos with the 100 billion galaxies, each with their 100 billion stars and associated planets, that our universe possesses. On the other hand, if the initial state were random, it ought to have been a high entropy mess, like the Big Crunch to which the simplest closed models tend. And inflation would not smooth out an initial mess. Indeed, Penrose is at pains to insist that there is a fundamental asymmetry between the Big Bang and Big Crunch, namely that the latter is highly disordered because of the second law of thermodynamics. In particular the irregularities of the Big Crunch would deviate dramatically from the symmetry of the standard FLRW models considered in Chapter 1. Inflation, says Penrose, "depends crucially on having an FLRW background (at least with regard to calculations that have actually been carried through)."[30] Our universe ought to resemble the time reversal of a Big Crunch, but is different from the Big Crunch to the astonishing degree we have been describing.

There is even worse to come. Indeed, as it stands, the multiverse proponent could simply say that if there were infinitely many universes embracing all possible starting configurations, then our highly ordered universe would be guaranteed to be among them. Penrose, however, points to the fact that for a universe to have life you actually need a great deal of order but much less than this vast amount.[31] You could create the entire solar system with all its planets and all its inhabitants by the random collisions of particles and radiation with a probability of 1 in $10^{10^{60}}$. This is a tiny probability but much greater than 1 in $10^{10^{123}}$ (looking at it the other way round, $10^{10^{123}}$ swamps $10^{10^{60}}$ entirely). The implication is that our universe is vastly more special than required merely in order for us to be here. It is much, much more special than a universe randomly selected from the subset of universes that are conducive to life. This is a very serious challenge for the multiverse idea but totally consistent with design.

Let us just press this argument a bit further. In order properly to appreciate it, we need to recognize that what is important is not the probability that a universe like ours exists, but the probability that we observe what we do, a point that has been emphasized by the philosopher Nick Bostrom.[32] If all possible universes exist, then of course ours exists with probability 1, but the probability of our observing such a universe is only 1 in $10^{10^{123}}$. According to Bostrom's formulation we should regard ourselves as typical observers in our reference class, and if we do that then we are vastly more likely to observe a small pocket of order surrounded by chaos than a totally ordered universe.

Ah, you may say, but there could be of the order of 10^{22} solar systems in our observable universe (roughly 10^{11} galaxies with roughly 10^{11} stars apiece). That would give 10^{22} times as many sentient beings as there are in our solar system, on the strong assumption, fair enough for these purposes, that each solar system produces sentient beings – and we should count ourselves in the reference class of sentient beings rather than humans per se. Certainly a highly ordered universe is likely to produce more sentient beings than any small pocket of order surrounded by chaos. Yet the fact is that it is far cheaper in terms of entropy to produce 10^{22} single solar systems surrounded by chaos than a single ordered universe with 10^{22} solar systems. There are $10^{10^{123}}$ times as many universes with one solar system as with 10^{22} solar systems, completely swamping the fact that the latter universes have 10^{22} times more inhabitants.

To summarize this point, if the multiverse explanation is correct, we ought to be in a universe with parameters just right for us but not vastly too special. The cosmological constant looks close to meeting this criterion, but the initial entropy of the universe fails catastrophically. There are other parameters that also look much too fine-tuned, again posing a problem for the multiverse hypothesis. The charge on the electron is fixed to eleven significant figures, but it could fluctuate by 1 part in 10^6 without affecting biochemistry, as pointed out by Paul Davies.[33] The lifetime of the proton is at least 2×10^{32} years, i.e. at least 10^{22} times the age of the universe, vastly longer than needed for life.[34]

So these two parameters look more special than is required simply for life and also pose a challenge to the multiverse hypothesis.

As we saw in Chapter 7, Penrose's own most recent model of the universe attempts to get over this problem by arguing that the universe, now conceived to be infinite, ultimately returns to its low entropy starting point (and not to a highly disordered Big Crunch). Penrose has not won many friends with this model, which is fraught with problems, both theoretical and observational. In any case it seems to me that the problem of why the universe possessed this very special cyclic property, with such an extraordinarily highly ordered beginning and end, would remain in any case, as would the problem of all the other fine-tunings. And, as we saw in Chapter 7, the standard infinite universe model would possess an even smaller (vanishingly small, in fact) probability of being ordered, compared with the finite Big Bang–Big Crunch model.

At the end of the next section I give an analogy which I trust will help elucidate the argument of these two sections.

8. Fine-Tuning for Embodied Conscious Agents

From the considerations of the previous section, and indeed from section 4 above as well, it looks as though we are not generic or typical observers in a multiverse. Rather, we are much more special observers than would be predicted by a multiverse model. Robin Collins takes this argument further.[35]

Collins first elucidates the point that we should indeed regard ourselves as typical or generic observers. He argues that, in order to do what is required of it, the multiverse hypothesis has to be combined with the "observer selection principle", the tautological claim that observers can only exist in a region of space–time in which the conditions, the constants that go into the laws of physics, and so on, are compatible with their existing. It is then supposed to be unsurprising that we as observers find ourselves in observer-structured regions of space–time since we could not exist in other types of region. That is also supposed to get round the problem that the multiverse renders what we ordinarily take to be improbable also unsurprising. For example, says Collins, we would normally say that it is too coincidental for someone to throw a die 50 times and get the number four every time. Yet in a large enough multiverse someone will indeed do that. The observer selection principle ensures that a randomly selected observer will do it with extremely low probability, and we should regard ourselves as randomly selected.

Collins then goes on to argue that, in a multiverse, "fluctuation observers" would be vastly more prevalent and therefore typical than the kind of observers we actually are. A fluctuation observer is rather like the observer mentioned in the previous section who lives in a solar system surrounded by chaos – a situation which could analogously be called a "fluctuation solar system". A fluctuation observer, then, is one who comes into being through the localized random collisions ("thermal fluctuations") of atoms and radiation, whereby the mass–energy in a small region moves from a state of disorder to high order (in terms of entropy, from high to low entropy). Fluctuation observers would be single, isolated, disembodied but self-aware entities – they would have just enough structure to have conscious experiences, and there would even be a proliferation of those with very similar conscious experiences to me, even though these experiences would for them be of a false reality.

This is all immensely improbable but will occur inevitably in a multiverse. Indeed fluctuation observers will occur many more times than whole solar systems containing observers. They will therefore also occur many, many more times than 10^{22} galaxies in a single region populated by as many observers as they have. Collins adds that such isolated fluctuation observers will exist in universes that are not fine-tuned. For example, if Λ were too large, observers like ourselves could not come into existence, but fluctuation observers would still be able to arise in the early part of the universe's expansion when thermal fluctuations would be occurring.

Fluctuation observers are also known as "Boltzmann brains". This terminology comes from the fact that the great Austrian physicist Ludwig Boltzmann put forward just this idea of thermal fluctuations to explain the existence of observers. However, it was pointed out to him, just as in the present discussion, that isolated islands of order incorporating Boltzmann brains would be far more numerous than whole ordered universes with creatures like ourselves.

Collins argues, then, that the universe is not in fact fine-tuned for observers. Rather, it is fine-tuned for what he calls embodied conscious agents (ECAs). ECAs are agents like ourselves who "can significantly interact with each other" and "can develop scientific technology and discover the universe". As an example, Collins cites the strength of gravity, which could in principle lie anywhere between zero and 10^{38} times its current value. However, when the strength of gravity is raised by a mere factor of 10 or 100 it becomes much more difficult for ECAs to function properly – for example, to build houses or do scientific experiments – and reducing the size of the planet brings other problems. So it looks as though ECAs like ourselves are very special indeed. (Note that in Chapter 5 we cited Collins elsewhere giving a possible range of zero to 10^{40} times its actual value for the strength of gravity, but this clearly makes negligible difference to the argument.)

Of course the multiverse advocate could put forward the same kind of response as the one to Penrose, which we considered in the last section. That is, fine-tuned universes might be much rarer than non fine-tuned ones, but they would contain many more observers. But, as above, the low probability of a fine-tuned universe compared with a non fine-tuned universe would completely swamp the fact that fine-tuned universes contain more observers. We are back to the conclusion that, if we regard ourselves as typical observers, we are utterly unlikely to belong to a community of similar observers able to interact morally and do science.

The following analogy may help to elucidate the argument presented above, and the arguments of sections 4 and 7. Imagine the proverbial monkey sitting at a computer and typing for trillions of years. Suppose that the monkey coming up with the lines "To be, or not to be, – that is the question" corresponds to a universe with observers in it. This will be very rare, but a monkey typing for an eternity will come up with this line from Hamlet infinitely many times (although, interestingly, in an experiment in 2002 a group of monkeys came nowhere near producing even a word, and much preferred to chew up the computer or use it as a lavatory![36]).

The problem is that we are not in a universe corresponding to "To be, or not to be, – that is the question," surrounded by meaningless rubbish. Rather we are in a universe that corresponds to the monkey coming up with the whole of Hamlet, or even the complete works of Shakespeare (Figure 8.1). The complete works of Shakespeare will also turn up eventually, and infinitely

Figure 8.1 Eventually the monkey will type "To be or not to be, – that is the question," but how long before he comes up with the complete works of Shakespeare?

many times, but nevertheless will be far, far rarer than just "To be, or not to be, – that is the question." We are far, far more likely to be in a "To be, or not to be, – that is the question" universe than a complete works of Shakespeare one. And that is a devastating problem for multiverses as an explanation for fine-tuning.

In contrast to the multiverse, the existence of God would render it unsurprising that a universe fine-tuned for ECAs exists and that we find ourselves in such a universe. Collins argues that God, considered to be perfectly good, as in classical Christian theism, would structure the universe so as to realize aesthetic and moral value.

Collins makes the further interesting point that theism is more conducive to the pursuit of science than the alternatives of either a single brute fact universe or a multiverse. He says that, because theism gives one confidence that the universe is discoverable, it can significantly impact one's scientific practice, for example in motivating the search for deeper theories in keeping with the aesthetic and moral value of the universe. He argues that atheism, by appealing to a multiverse, can be a "science stopper". This is in direct contrast to what is asserted by militant atheists such as Richard Dawkins, that religious belief is a science stopper: "If you don't understand how something works, never mind: just give up and say God did it."[37] This relates to my point in section 4 above, that surprising things may occur in the laboratory to which a multiverse proponent can simply react by saying, "We just happen to be in a universe which exhibits that phenomenon."

Theism as a Motivation for Scientific Discovery

As an example of theism providing a motivation for scientific discovery, Collins cites the extra, seemingly superfluous, generations of quarks and leptons. All ordinary matter is composed of two types of quark ("up" and "down") and two types of lepton (the electron and electron neutrino), yet there exist three generations of each of these, seemingly irrelevant for life. Collins says the existence of these extra generations might signify some deeper, more elegant theory, or they might have some indirect relevance to life. Either way, theism would provide a reason for their existence, and a motivation to search for that reason, whereas a multiverse theory would not: such things just would occur in some universe or other. We could call this a "multiverse of the gaps" as opposed to the "God of the gaps" derided by Dawkins – a view of God which is in any case deeply flawed theologically as well as liable to be undermined by the progress of science.

Another example Collins gives relates to the cosmological constant. As we saw above, the value of Λ could not be enormously larger than it is and remain compatible with life. However, if it were smaller than it is, it would be undetectable, and it could perfectly well be zero and still be compatible with a life-bearing universe, as in the Einstein–de Sitter model. As we saw in Chapter 1, Einstein came to see Λ as ugly and regretted having included it in his equations in the first place. If it were indeed inelegant, then the theist would be motivated to find a reason why it takes a detectable value and whether it points to some deeper theory.

---

9. The Prevalence of Fake Universes

Given a multiverse, it turns out that we are much more likely to be in a fake universe, simulated by some super-intelligence, rather as portrayed in the 1999 science fiction film *The Matrix*, than in a real universe. That is because, as Paul Davies says, as soon as we even entertain the possibility of a multiverse, there seems no good reason to rule out universes that contain computer simulations of other universes. Indeed, in a multiverse, technological civilizations like ours will emerge in some subset of universes, and civilizations more technologically advanced than ours will attain the capacity to simulate consciousness. As Davies says, "It is but a small step from simulating consciousness to simulating a community of conscious beings and an entire virtual world for them to inhabit."[38]

The philosopher Nick Bostrom argues that our own post-human descendants might well have immense computing power and therefore the capacity to run a great many such simulations.[39] We could thus be simulations of the human ancestors of post-humans, rather than real humans. And, of course, we would be but one example of an intelligent civilization in the multiverse. So, with some reasonable estimates of the numbers and probabilities involved, Bostrom concludes that such simulations are likely to be overwhelmingly dominant among universes as a whole. A random observer would thus be far more likely to find himself in a simulation than a real universe. Given once again that we should regard ourselves as typical observers, we should therefore conclude that our universe is much more likely to be a simulation than a real universe, and we are therefore not real biological persons but simulated ones. So argues Bostrom, and Paul Davies concurs. John Barrow makes the same point.[40] And, of course, these are a serious philosopher, based in Oxford, and two of the world's most eminent cosmologists, based in Arizona and Cambridge!

If this isn't bizarre enough, both Davies and Barrow note some even more bizarre features of this scenario. First the computer programmers creating the simulations resemble God in some respects and can create arbitrary laws, or act miraculously or capriciously – indeed do anything they please – to interfere with the simulations they have created. Furthermore, simulations, or the capricious "gods" within them, can spawn simulations and other "gods" ad infinitum. If this is ultimate reality, argues Davies, the idea of a rationally ordered universe is false and science becomes pointless. And, as Barrow observes, "If most of these worlds are virtual, then they can display illusory laws of physics and we are on a slippery slope to knowing nothing at all because there is no reliable knowledge to be had."[41]

The reader may by now think we are entering the realm of the surreal. Indeed, rather than entertaining this quite bizarre possibility – surely a *reductio ad absurdum* of the multiverse hypothesis – surely the simpler position to adopt, as with all these problems, is the theistic one. That is to say, there is one super-intelligence, the unique necessary being of traditional Christian theology, who because he is perfectly good and trustworthy (and not capricious) creates one, real universe, with real creatures in it who have the capacity to understand its workings.

Bearing in mind all the problems I have now outlined, I shall go on in the next two chapters to compare the possible explanations for fine-tuning. The multiverse is problematic, but does the theistic explanation fare any better? My aim is to show that it does indeed.

9

COMPARING THE EXPLANATIONS

When it was proclaimed that the Library contained all books, the first impression was one of extravagant happiness. All men felt themselves to be the masters of an intact and secret treasure. There was no personal or world problem whose eloquent solution did not exist in some hexagon. The universe was justified, the universe suddenly usurped the unlimited dimensions of hope... As was natural, this inordinate hope was followed by an excessive despair. The certitude that some shelf in some hexagon held precious books and that these precious books were inaccessible, seemed almost intolerable. A blasphemous sect suggested that the searchers should cease and that all men should juggle letters and symbols until they constructed, by an improbable gift of chance, these canonical books. The authorities were obliged to issue severe orders. The sect disappeared, but in my childhood I have seen old men who, for long periods of time, would hide in the latrines with some metal disks in a forbidden dice cup and feebly mimic the divine disorder.

Jorge Luis Borges (1941)[1]

God v. Multiverse

How can we choose between the multiverse explanation without God and divine design? In the last chapter I listed a host of problems with the multiverse explanation in addition to the fact that no purely physical explanation will ever be ultimate. So here are just a few of the problems again by way of summary:

1. A multiverse doesn't provide an ultimate explanation. One can always ask, "Why is there something rather than nothing?"

2. It is also a complex explanation. Simpler explanations involving the least number of entities and kinds of entities are preferred in general in science, so scientists ought to be sceptical about the gigantic multiplication of entities involved in multiverse theories. There is also the question, for any particular multiverse, "Why does this particular multiverse exist and not another?"

3. A multiverse doesn't explain why there should be life. There is no reason in principle why a multiverse should do so. The question is always, "Why does this particular set of laws, which gives rise to the multiverse in question, give rise to life?"

4. This universe looks too special. It is more special than is required for life, or observers, to develop, and this speaks of design more than of any kind of random selection.

Why does God provide a superior explanation to the multiverse? Is not the theistic hypothesis equally full of problems? To answer these questions, let me first say something about what I mean by God. Indeed, Leonard Susskind challenged me to do just that at the symposium in Stanford I referred to in Chapter 7. At that symposium, Paul Davies, the joint chair with Andrei Linde, had asked the string theorists to make their presentations intelligible to non-specialists. So Susskind's immediate challenge to me was the *tu quoque*, "What do you mean by God?"

I take the term "God" to mean a being who transcends the physical universe – he is above and beyond space and time. He possesses unlimited power. He instantiates the laws of physics, first making a choice among possible laws. He is thus not subject to the laws of physics; rather they are subject to him. God upholds the laws of nature with which he has endowed the universe, though he is not constrained by them. As St Augustine wrote at the beginning of the fifth century:

> God has established in the temporal order fixed laws governing the production of kinds of beings and qualities of beings and bringing them forth from a hidden state into full view, but His will is supreme over all. By His power He has given numbers to His creation, but He has not bound His power by these numbers.[2]

God is not subject to the laws of physics. However, he is subject to the laws of logic. That must be so if "God" is to be a coherent concept. Not even God can make the statements A and ~A (meaning "not A") simultaneously true. One of the most important properties he possesses from the point of view of the argument of this book is that he is "necessary", meaning that he cannot but exist, or he exists in all possible worlds. To say that God is a necessary being is to stipulate, at least in part, what we mean by the term "God". God shares this necessity with the laws of logic and of mathematics, but not with the laws of physics or with the physical universe. We have seen this latter point in our discussion of Chapter 4 where we contrasted the necessity of God with the contingency of the universe.

It will be noted that I have used the pronoun "he" to refer to God. Thus God is also personal, but it must be acknowledged, as St Thomas Aquinas argued, that all talk about God uses the language of analogy. Our statements about God bear some resemblance to statements made in the human realm, but also differ from those statements. In the past the pronoun "he" has been taken to be a personal pronoun that embraces both genders. The pronoun "she" indicated a feminine person. The latter is still true, but now "he" is often taken to be masculine, leaving us with no generic singular personal pronoun. This problem is often avoided by not using a pronoun at all but always referring to "God" and "Godself", a usage which I find cumbersome. In addition, in the Christian tradition Jesus has taught us to pray "Our Father", again analogous language, and also taking us into the particulars of revelation, which are beyond where the kind of argument advanced in this book can get us. To complicate matters further, the Christian tradition also understands God to have revealed himself as Trinity – Father, Son, and Holy Spirit – also making the use of the singular personal pronoun somewhat problematic. While I believe the findings of science to be entirely consonant with the Christian revelation, including the relationality of the persons of the Trinity, and that there are good reasons for believing in the triune God, I do not intend to press that case here, for to do so would take us way beyond the scope of this book.[3] In summary, for the purposes of this chapter, the conception of God needed is that common to the Abrahamic faiths, and not particular to Christianity, and I retain the pronoun "he" for convenience.

Theism is an unpopular hypothesis for many scientists. They want to confine their explanations to within science itself. To step outside the closed system of scientific law and postulate an all-powerful being, who is not amenable to scientific study, is anathema. On the other hand, doing science at all entails making assumptions of a metaphysical kind, e.g. that there is order out there to be found in nature, and that the laws uncovered are universal, operating right across the whole space–time universe. Making such assumptions is justified retrospectively because science is successful, but Christians would want to say that belief in God as giver of order justifies these assumptions. The idea that humans are made in the image of God explains why we can understand the universe and do science. Medieval theologians expressed this in terms of *adaequatio intellectus ad rem* – the adequation of the intellect to reality, or the match between our cognitive faculties and the world, as philosopher Alvin Plantinga expresses it.[4] Georges Lemaître, the Father of the Big Bang, captured this idea beautifully when, in a popular survey of his cosmology, he wrote this:

> We cannot end this rapid review which we have made together of the most magnificent subject that the human mind may be tempted to explore without being proud of these splendid endeavours of Science in the conquest of the Earth, and also without expressing our gratitude to One Who has said: "I am the Truth", One Who gave us the mind to understand Him and to recognize a glimpse of His glory in our universe which He has so wonderfully adjusted to the mental power with which He has endowed us.[5]

Christians would also say that belief in God is founded on much more than the classic so-called "proofs" debated by philosophers. Cumulative case arguments for the existence of God, which take account of many strands of evidence, have been pioneered in recent decades by philosophers such as Basil Mitchell and Richard Swinburne.[6]

In contrast to the multiverse, creation and design of the universe by God provides an ultimate explanation because God, if he exists, exists necessarily. In addition, design by God is a simple explanation and much more economical than the multiverse. One is not invoking a whole multitude of complex entities with which one can have no possible interaction, but one intelligent being, like ourselves in some ways but so much greater, who designed the universe with the deliberate intention of its bringing forth creatures for a relationship with himself. Christians would argue that, not only is there no reason in principle why God should not have observable effects in the world he has made, but that there are purported effects to be investigated (one might cite the historical claims made for the life, death, and resurrection of Christ, and the claims of many to have experienced God in their lives, though again all this takes us way beyond what can be discussed in a book on the Big Bang[7]).

Design by God explains why there should be intelligent life and why the universe should be special, even extra special as we find it. That is because it is the good creation of an all-powerful, all-knowing, perfectly good being. Is not modern cosmology pointing to God as designer?

Making the Comparison Rigorous

We can make the argument of the preceding section more rigorous by elucidating some criteria for one explanation being superior to another, and seeing how theism and the multiverse without God compare. We have focused so far on the ability of a hypothesis to explain the evidence in question, and we shall have more to say about that. In the jargon of probability theory, it is measured by the *likelihood* of the hypothesis, i.e. the probability that the evidence pertains given that the hypothesis is true. But a second very important consideration is the implicit plausibility of the hypothesis even before the evidence is examined. This is measured by the *prior probability* that the hypothesis is true.

There is a theorem in probability theory, discovered by the Revd Thomas Bayes in the eighteenth century, which tells us how to derive the probability that the hypothesis is true given we see the evidence in question. This latter probability, which is what we really want to know, is called the *posterior probability* of the hypothesis. It depends on the prior probability, the likelihood of the hypothesis, and the likelihood of the negation of the hypothesis. This last likelihood is the probability that we see the evidence when the hypothesis is false.

The formula for Bayes's theorem is given in the Appendix, together with illustrative calculations using it. I shall now give these examples here in the main text, but simply summarize the results without going into the mathematics.[8]

Suppose, first, that 1 per cent of the population suffer from a certain disease that lies dormant for many years before becoming quickly fatal. There is a diagnostic test that gives the following results. If a person has the disease, the test is positive 90 per cent of the time. If a person does not have the disease, the test shows positive 10 per cent of the time.

I hear about this disease on television and become extremely anxious, although I have no symptoms. I decide to go to my doctor and ask for the test. It is positive.

In the language of probability theory, the prior probability that I have the disease is 1 per cent. The likelihood of the hypothesis that I have it is 90 per cent. The likelihood of the negation of the hypothesis, i.e. the hypothesis that I don't have it, is 10 per cent.

If asked what the probability is that I have the disease, given that the test is positive, most people would say 90 per cent, which is to confuse the posterior probability with the likelihood. However, a straightforward application of Bayes's theorem, as shown in the Appendix, shows that the posterior probability is in fact 1/12, which ought to be somewhat reassuring. An alternative way of expressing this is to say that it is eleven times more likely that I don't have the disease than that I do, or that the "odds" are eleven to one against my having it.

From this example, we can see how taking account of the evidence (the test is positive) has raised the probability that I have the disease, from its prior value of 1/100 to its posterior value of 1/12. The probability that I do not have the disease has correspondingly been reduced from 99/100 to 11/12.

Here is a second example. One dark and rainy night Sarah witnesses a hit-and-run accident. The car involved in the accident is a taxi, and Sarah tells the police that it was blue. There are two taxi firms in the town, one using green taxis and the other blue taxis. The green taxi firm is the dominant one with 85 per cent of the taxis. Sarah is tested to see if she can correctly identify the colours of taxis under similar conditions to the night in question, and she is right 80 per cent of the time. The jury is asked to judge whether it was indeed a blue taxi, as reported, which committed the crime.[9]

In this example, the prior probability that the culprit was driving a blue taxi is 15 per cent, i.e. 0.15; the likelihood that it was blue, i.e. the probability that it was reported blue if it was blue is 0.8; the likelihood that it was green is 0.2. The correct answer to this problem contradicts what most psychological tests reveal people's judgments to be. As in the case of the diagnostic test, many people confuse the likelihood, the probability that it was reported blue given that it was blue, with the posterior probability, the probability that it was indeed blue given that it was reported as blue. Most people think the criminal in this example was more likely to have been driving a blue car. However, Bayes's theorem shows that the posterior probability that the car was blue, given the report that it was blue, is only about 0.41. Thus, despite a fairly reliable witness testifying to it being blue, it is in reality more likely to have been a green car.

The fact that we are inclined to misjudge probabilities is rather worrying for the jury system in Britain, where, in a notable case, the Appeal Court ended up deciding that experts should not explain Bayes's theorem to juries or guide them through the process of using it. Peter Donnelly of Oxford University has described how this could be done without baffling juries with mathematics.[10]

The Explanatory Options

When it comes to evaluating the theistic hypothesis against alternatives, things are a little trickier than the rather neat and tidy examples given above. It is much more difficult to know what probabilities to put into Bayes's theorem when comparing metaphysical hypotheses. However, we can give reasons for assigning a much higher prior probability to one hypothesis rather than another and to the probabilities of seeing particular pieces of evidence given one hypothesis rather than another (the likelihoods). The rationale for doing this in the first place is that we believe that the probability of a single universe randomly chosen from the set of possible universes being fine-tuned is minute indeed, and that a multiverse supposedly raises the probability of the existence of fine-tuned universes. In a nutshell, the probability framework is essentially a way of making more informal judgments rigorous and self-consistent. Scientists themselves make "inferences to the best explanation" by comparing the relative simplicity, elegance, and scope of competing hypotheses, and the probability framework formalizes such an approach.[11]

Figure 9.1 shows the two main options. The first option is that God chooses a theory into which he breathes fire. There are a vast number to choose from, all of which exist in the mind of God. God makes his choice with the intention of bringing about rational creatures who are capable of many things, but above all of having a relationship with him. That will affect his choice of theory. It will affect how many times the theory is instantiated. He will very likely choose a theory that describes a highly ordered cosmos. It is not impossible that he create a multiverse, though I think there is a lot of work for theologians to do if it becomes evident that a multiverse really exists, and my metaphysical and theological preference[12] would be for a single universe (of course, if one adopted the God *and* multiverse position, one would need to consider what kind of multiverse God might create). But theology does respond to challenges, and issues of human identity, free will, and the need or not for multiple incarnations, are some of those which would need to be addressed.[13]

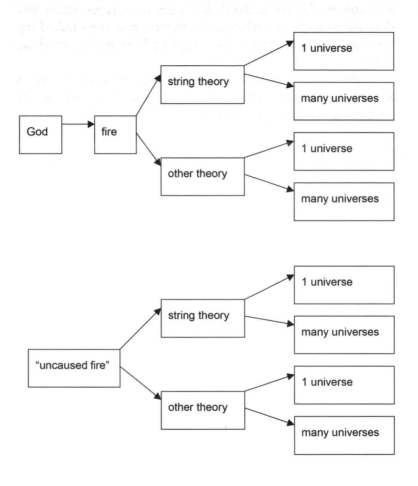

Figure 9.1 The explanatory options.

The second option is that some theory is instantiated without God's involvement: we could say that "uncaused fire" lights up a particular theory or set of theories, giving rise to a single universe or many universes. A priori there is not much to choose between theories or realizations of universes except on grounds of simplicity. Unlike in the theistic case, there is no reason why the choice should be anthropically skewed. And the whole thing has to get off the ground in the first place. Why is there anything at all?

In the next chapter, we show how Bayes's theorem can indeed elucidate the comparison between explanatory hypotheses for the fine-tuning in a rigorous way.

10

THEISM WINS

I want to know how God created this world. I'm not interested in this or that phenomenon, in the spectrum of this or that element. I want to know His thoughts; the rest are details.

Albert Einstein (1955)[1]

The Prior Probabilities

We now embark on making the arguments considered hitherto more rigorous by using Bayes's theorem, introduced in the last chapter. For the mathematically minded, the calculations are given in the Appendix. For convenience, we restrict ourselves to two explanatory options: (1) God creates a single universe fine-tuned for us to be in it; and (2) there is no God but there is an uncaused multiverse. Thus we have excluded from consideration the idea that God creates a multiverse, which is of course possible and which some Christians believe to be the case, and we have excluded a single brute fact universe that just happens to be fine-tuned. It is reasonable to exclude the last option because its utter improbability is what has motivated the multiverse in the first place.

First, then, let us consider the prior probabilities. The main criterion we have for comparing the priors is simplicity. Simplicity is a difficult concept to make precise, but it is regularly used in science to choose between competing hypotheses that explain the same data. Other things being equal, a hypothesis that is simpler than a rival is likely to have a higher prior probability.

Richard Swinburne considers as an example Newton's inverse square law of gravitation, which says that the gravitational force between two bodies is inversely proportional to the square of the distance between them. That is to say, the gravitational force varies as $1/r^2$, where r is the distance between the two bodies. Swinburne suggests that an inverse square law is simpler than an inverse $2.00 \dots$ (100 zeros) $\dots 01$ power law and therefore more likely to be true.[2] The latter is both unnatural and would have physically unsatisfying consequences. Moreover, there are infinitely many numbers to choose from, close to 2 and within a small range of it, which would be compatible with experiment. At the very least, it has been of immense pragmatic value to choose a $1/r^2$ law rather than a $1/r^{2.00 \dots (100 \text{ zeros}) \dots 01}$ one. If the experimental evidence were compatible with both these laws, the scientist would invariably opt for the $1/r^2$ law. To choose a $1/r^{2.00 \dots (100 \text{ zeros}) \dots 01}$ law would seem very ad hoc and indeed irrational.

One of the most significant ways in which a hypothesis is simpler than a rival is if it postulates fewer entities and kinds of entities. For example, a theory that postulated fewer kinds of fundamental particles would be simpler than one that postulated many, and so, again, more likely a priori to be true. This is captured in the principle of Ockham's razor, which states that "entities are not to be multiplied beyond necessity."

To begin with, let us think about the multiverse (together with the non-existence of God). The following argument applies, or can be adapted, to any version of the multiverse, but for the sake of definiteness let us have the string theory version in mind. The prior probability of the string theory multiverse is arguably very low because it is not a simple hypothesis. The hypothesis violates the principle of Ockham's razor in a most extravagant way. There are plenty of simpler hypotheses around. To raise its probability one would need to be assured that string theory has observational consequences *and* that there are good reasons to suppose that the maximal version of what is allowed in string/M-theory is instantiated. At present, neither of these criteria is met.

There is also a problem if certain parameters need to be fine-tuned so that a multiverse arises, since fine-tuning is what the multiverse is invoked to explain in the first place. Also, why string theory at all? Why this particular multiverse generator? Indeed, why this particular subset of possible universes from Tegmark's grand ensemble? Of course, the same questions would arise if we had chosen to focus on some other multiverse model.

Given that there is a selection anyway, the a priori probability of a particular multiverse must reflect the large number of options. Yet we are in a cleft stick because the probability of the whole "anything possible exists" multiverse is the most violently anti-Ockhamite of all, and barely, if at all, coherent (see the careful analysis of Stoeger *et al.*[3]). It is also worth adding the considerations I gave in Chapter 4 concerning the contingency of any physical universe existing at all.

Now cosmologist Paul Davies also believes that God is a complex hypothesis, just about as complex as the standard multiverse model.[4] Richard Dawkins argues that invoking God to explain "organized complexity" fails because God has to be more complex than what he is explaining.[5] Dawkins seems to think that organized complexity can only come about through Darwinian evolution. Of course no theologian, or indeed Christian believer, has ever thought God came about at all, let alone by evolution. And in any case Dawkins' concept of organized complexity is about the physical arrangement of material parts and is completely irrelevant to the concept of God. One has only to consult Article 1 of the Church of England's Thirty-Nine Articles of Religion to see a classical theistic statement on the concept of God: "There is but one living and true God, everlasting, without body, parts, or passions; of infinite power, wisdom, and goodness; the Maker, and Preserver of all things both visible and invisible."

Traditionally theologians have thought of God as simple. For example, Aquinas argued that God is simple because he is necessary, because he cannot change, because, in fact, his properties of omnipotence, omniscience, and perfect goodness inhere in God necessarily. God is thus unlike everything else we can conceive. And, in addition, his being without a body or parts, let alone organized physical parts, makes him simple.

God's simplicity has been argued for in recent years by Richard Swinburne.[6] Swinburne argues that God is simple because, for example, he possesses unlimited power (as of course he does in the classical view). He is simple because he can both create and mould matter, unlike Plato's demiurge who was limited to moulding pre-existent matter. Unlimited power (constrained only by logic) is simpler than some finite amount. There is an analogy here with the way that in science a $1/r^2$ law is so much more natural and therefore much simpler than a $1/r^{2.00 \ldots (100 \text{ zeros}) \ldots 01}$ law. If there were some limit on God's power, one would have to ask why the limit was just at that point and not some other. Given there are an infinite number of ways in which God's power might be limited, the particular cut-off point for God's power, if there were one, would inevitably be arbitrary and immensely improbable.

In a similar way, the hypothesis of one God is vastly simpler than the hypothesis of many gods. If there were many gods, one would have to ask, "Why this number and not another?" and each possible number would be immensely improbable.

The philosopher William Lane Craig also argues for the simplicity of God. He makes the point, again in line with the classical position noted above, that a mind is simple, being an immaterial entity not composed of parts. The contents of a mind may be complex, but not the mind itself.[7] Patrick Richmond is another author who has argued that God's mind is simple, not being composed of many parts, thus defeating Richard Dawkins' argument for God's immense improbability.[8] Richmond's is a careful analysis of the issues, and treats

Dawkins' argument with the seriousness he thinks it deserves.

Swinburne doesn't take God to be necessary (which I think somewhat strange), but I believe that God's necessity, which has been traditionally argued for (in contrast to the necessity of any physical universe) enhances the prior probability of theism. Anyway, if one accepts the argument then the prior probability of God will be much greater than that of the string theory multiverse; if not the probabilities could be comparable, as Paul Davies believes.

The philosopher Eleonore Stump also believes that Swinburne's argument would be much strengthened if he were to take God as a logically necessary being, just as Aquinas does.[9] As it stands, there are various points at which a sceptic might find Swinburne's argument unpersuasive – his definition of simplicity, his claim that God is the simplest person, that he is a simpler object than a physical universe, and that therefore his existence is simpler than that of a physical universe. But if one added simplicity to God's attributes and utilized Aquinas's technical definition of simplicity, these difficulties would evaporate. For, on Aquinas's definition, God's simplicity implies that God is identical with his existence, meaning that God is logically necessary. And then it *is* the case that theism is a simpler hypothesis than a multiverse, or indeed the existence of any physical universe, as the stopping point for explanation. This is because, as we discussed earlier, the question, "Why is there something rather than nothing?" is just not answered at all in the latter case. Theism alone provides the ultimate explanation.

Of course, if God is logically necessary, then the probability of his existence is 1. However, what we are talking about here is the "epistemic probability" rather than the objective or logical probability. In fact, the logical probability is either 1 or 0. The latter would be right if God were not logically necessary and did not in fact exist: God either exists or he doesn't, and there is no halfway house. The epistemic probability, however, is that based on "rational degree of belief", the degree of belief it is rationally appropriate to assign to a proposition, and that can certainly lie between 0 and 1.

As an illustration of this point, let us consider Goldbach's conjecture in mathematics. This states that every even integer greater than 2 can be expressed as the sum of two prime numbers. An example would be $8 = 3 + 5$. The problem is that Goldbach's conjecture, extremely simple to state as it is, has never been proved from the axioms of mathematics. Hence, although the conjecture has objective probability either 1 or 0 (it is either true or false), we should exercise due caution and refrain from giving it an epistemic probability of 1 – quite high, perhaps, since no counter-example has been discovered, but not quite 1, which would indicate that it is true with absolute certainty.

An important question that arises for this view of God is, "How can a necessary being create a contingent universe?" Isn't it the case that a necessary being must create necessarily and must create a unique world (perhaps "the best of all possible worlds", though such a concept is problematical)? That would make the world God makes necessary and so, the argument goes, we are back to square one with a necessary world, so making the necessary being redundant. This is a problem which troubles Paul Davies, for example.[10] It is precisely because he thinks, conversely, that the universe is contingent and that a contingent universe can only be made by a logically contingent being that Richard Swinburne rejects the notion of God as possessing logically necessary existence.

Stump makes the point, however, that for orthodox Christians (as opposed, for example, to neo-Platonists, for whom the universe is an emanation flowing ineluctably from the divine being) the universe is created by an act of God's free will. The universe is dependent not just on God's logically necessary being but on acts of his free, i.e. logically contingent, will.

Keith Ward also argues that God must have both necessary and contingent properties, and provides a detailed argument as to how this is so and how this defeats the argument troubling

Swinburne, Davies, and others.[11] Ward begins from Anselm's definition, pre-dating Aquinas's arguments about God's necessity by a century and a half, that God is "that than which nothing greater can be conceived". Such a being will necessarily possess maximal power and supreme value. An omnipotent being will necessarily be the Creator of everything other than itself, since otherwise there would exist something over which it did not exercise power, and there will necessarily be only one such being. God, then, is necessarily omnipotent and necessarily good.

So far, so good. But then the question arises, "Why does God create?" The simplest answer is that God desires the good and so wills to bring about good states. But if God's desires are necessary (and it would certainly seem to be necessary that he desires the good), then the universe acquires the sort of necessity which we saw was problematic above.

Ward, however, makes the point that, while the set of possibilities (possible universes) is necessarily what it is, the set of actually existing universes is contingent. Even God cannot make the possibilities other than what they are. However, he may freely choose which of those possibilities to make actual, and, according to the Christian tradition, does indeed freely create out of love, just as Stump says. In particular, the concept of the "best of all possible worlds", which God would necessarily create, is incoherent – or at any rate there is no such thing. This is for a similar reason to that which makes "infinitely many universes" problematic, namely that one could always add to any given amount of goodness which a world possesses. The amount of goodness a world can possess is unlimited.

Ward argues that God's goodness does not constrain God, who remains omnipotent. He creates out of his overflowing love, yet not by necessity since, Christians would argue, perfect love flows eternally between the persons of the Trinity. God does not need the world, at least according to classical theism.

In considering the range of possible goods, Ward notes that some goods cannot be realized simultaneously, e.g. the whole of a Beethoven symphony; different goods are incommensurate, making comparison impossible, e.g. listening to a Beethoven symphony and going for a walk in the country; and for many goods the continuing creative process in realizing rich new created possibilities involves patiently waiting as they evolve and develop, and interacting with them as they do so. It follows that even God cannot possess all goods simultaneously and therefore *must* make a choice. (Note that even if God could enjoy two humanly incompatible goods at once, he couldn't enjoy *me* enjoying them.)

It follows from all this that God possesses both necessary and contingent properties. He possesses dispositional properties that are necessary, such as the capacity to enjoy the good. But his actual possession of any particular good is contingent, since the set of actualized goods continually changes. Likewise God's power is a necessary dispositional property, namely the disposition to bring about whatever good states God desires, but the actual exercise of God's power is contingent on the specific circumstances obtaining at a particular time.

More simply, God's omnipotence logically entails that he possess both necessary and contingent properties because, if God could not create a contingent world, there would be a great many things he could not do and he would therefore not be omnipotent. It is quite interesting that discussions of the problems surrounding the realization of multiverses (such as Tegmark's and the possibilities considered by Ellis *et al.*) are not far from the surface when we consider the distinctions between necessary and contingent divine properties! To me it seems that the position outlined by Ward is entirely coherent, and there is no contradiction between God subsisting as necessary being and his creating a contingent universe (or multiverse).

The upshot of what you may regard as these rather complex arguments about simplicity is that God is simple compared with a multiverse. The God hypothesis should therefore be accorded a much greater prior probability than the multiverse hypothesis.

If you do not accept the arguments, it would seem reasonable to opt for Paul Davies' position that God and a multiverse are, a priori, just about equally complex and therefore just about equally improbable.

The Likelihoods

Moving on, then, from the prior probabilities, what can we say about the likelihoods that go into Bayes's theorem? Remember that the prior probability of a hypothesis is the probability that the hypothesis is true before the evidence is taken into account; the likelihood of the hypothesis is the probability that the evidence would pertain given that the hypothesis were true; and what we are after is the posterior probability, which tells us how we should revise our prior probability in the light of the evidence (it is the probability that the hypothesis is true given the evidence).

For some of the reasons given in Chapter 8 it would seem that the string landscape, like other multiverse scenarios, by no means guarantees that our universe (or any life-supporting one) would exist. Of course, if one is essentially starting from a universe of our type with our kind of physical laws, and postulating that the constants take on many different values in different universes, that will raise the probability above what it would have been in the single universe case. However, the probability that a fine-tuned universe exists could still be quite low, precisely because one has preselected a theory that ostensibly applies to our universe, into which fire is breathed (string theory), and thus one has chosen a universe-generating mechanism that prejudices the chosen multiverse towards producing life. But there are many, many possible multiverses, the vast majority of which will be dead and lifeless. The probability that a multiverse chosen at random from the set of multiverses contains fine-tuned members would be low. (There are, in fact, some technical mathematical difficulties here to do with how you translate proportions into probabilities and to do with realizable infinities,[12] but these do not alter this fundamental conclusion, taken as a judgment of "epistemic probability".)

Now you might think that the probability of there being a fine-tuned universe would be higher the more comprehensive a theory is. So it would be 1 for Tegmark's grand ensemble in which all possible universes exist, if one makes the additional assumption that universes which arise from the instantiation of all possible mathematical structures exhaust the possibilities – which is not obvious. It is worth noting, however, as has been pointed out by Keith Ward, that if all possible universes exist, then it follows that God exists.[13] The "maximal multiverse", if invoked to remove the need for God, has the directly opposite consequence! This is because a version of the so-called "ontological argument" now comes into play. If God is possible, then there is a possible universe in which God exists as its Creator. But the maximal multiverse makes that possible universe actually exist. Therefore God exists. But since God is necessary, it follows that God exists in all possible (and, *ex hypothesi*, existent) universes – that is the meaning of the term "necessary". Obviously, in particular, God then exists as Creator of our universe.

In addition, what you gain in explanatory power by invoking the maximal multiverse is lost in simplicity and hence in the prior probability – the Tegmark multiverse is maximally anti-Ockhamite, so the prior is low. We saw in Chapter 8 that Tim Mawson does not regard the maximal multiverse as complex. But, even if that is correct, there is a much more serious point, which undermines any of the multiverse theories on offer. While it is true that some observer in some universe would observe the fine-tuning we actually do (that is guaranteed in the maximal multiverse case), it is not the case that our observing it is at all probable, for reasons which go back to our discussion of Penrose, Collins, and Mawson himself in Chapter 8. It depends on whether or not we are observing anything too special for our existence. If Penrose is right, the probability that we observe the order we do is 1 in $10^{10^{123}}$. We are much more likely to find ourselves in an ordered solar system surrounded by complete disorder. Similarly, following Collins, we should regard ourselves as generic observers and as such we are vastly more likely to be Boltzmann brains than fully embodied conscious agents as we are, with the capacity to do science and dwelling in a universe so remarkably adapted for us to do so. And Mawson argues that it is vastly improbable that the principle of induction should work, and go on working, in our universe. Thus the probability that we observe what we do is so low as to be almost vanishingly small.

Now, of course, on the theistic hypothesis God has a lot of options and may not make this particular universe. However, there are very good reasons for him to want to make a universe something like this one – with rational creatures in it able to enjoy a relationship with him, and extra special so that they can understand and learn about the universe in which they have been placed. Hence the probability of us observing what we do should be vastly higher than on the multiverse hypothesis. Indeed, again if Penrose is right, any reasonably moderate values of the other terms in Bayes's theorem will be annihilated by the utterly minuscule probability that we observe the wonderfully ordered universe that we do. So, even if we take Paul Davies' judgment that a multiverse and theism are equally complex and so equally (im)probable, we should still vastly prefer theism over the multiverse. That is because, when we combine the prior probabilities with the likelihoods using Bayes's theorem, as shown in the Appendix, the almost negligibly small likelihood of the multiverse hypothesis completely dominates the other factors.

Even if we feel it is impossible to make any kind of judgment at all about the prior probabilities – and this is the most controversial aspect of the argument – it is still rational to conclude that the multiverse hypothesis fails catastrophically to explain the data, and the theistic hypothesis (however intrinsically (im)probable) does explain it.

Where is Science Going?

My argument has been that the fine-tuning is best explained by Christian theism. It is an argument from nature to God, an exercise in "natural theology". An interesting question is: can one go the other way, in the sense that if one were to come to cosmology with a prior commitment to the traditional Christian theology of creation, would that make a difference to one's science? It is certainly a risky business telling scientists what they will find from prior ideological commitments of any sort. We have seen that with atheism and the perfect cosmological principle, and of course creationists make a big mistake here; and I am wary of theology making predictions as theologian Nancey Murphy, for example, would have it do.[14] But it is interesting that the Christian doctrine of creation gave the impetus to scientific discovery in Western Christendom in the first place, because it said that the universe was freely created by God as totally distinct from God, and is therefore contingent, as I have discussed at length. That means that the only way to find out about the universe is to carry out experiments and observations. And we have seen how Robin Collins thinks that theism provides greater motivation towards scientific discovery than the multiverse.

It seems that there is a move away from experiment and observation at the present time, especially with string theory and the multiverse. Science seems to be retreating from the universe being contingent to its being necessary, if not in the sense of existing necessarily, then of necessarily taking the form it does given that it exists, because everything that can happen does happen somewhere some time in some universe. That seems to be departing from the Christian view of the contingency of the universe but also departing from the scientific method, which was a response to the Christian doctrine. Should not cosmology and theology be coming close together again at this point?

Coming back to my main point, in summary, in light of all the problems I have identified, is not creation and design by

God the best explanation for the existence of the universe and its very special characteristics? Do we not live in "a universe designed for life"?

Concluding Remarks

What I have presented here, as I draw this book to a close, is, I believe, a powerful argument for the existence of God. The theistic hypothesis explains why there should be intelligent life and why the universe should be special, even extra special as we find it. That is because it is the good creation of an all-powerful, all-knowing, perfectly good being.

That is of course only the beginning. But it is I trust a starting point from which to explore the particularities of faith, and in particular the events surrounding the life, death, and resurrection of Jesus Christ. These too can be explored on an evidential and rational basis, just as the issue of God's existence has been explored with reference to one particular strand of evidence in this book. Sooner or later, however, any enquirer will be faced with the existential decision: how do I live my life? Do I go on exploring these issues from the outside as an intellectual exercise, sitting on the fence? Or do I take the step of faith – not irrational faith but "faith seeking understanding", as Anselm put it – and start, perhaps tentatively, exploring from inside the community of faith? It is my hope and prayer that the honest enquirer will be enabled to go beyond the abstract nature and technical difficulties of philosophical argument and to affirm, with St Paul, that

> for us there is one God, the Father, from whom are all things and for whom we exist, and one Lord, Jesus Christ, through whom are all things and through whom we exist. (1 Corinthians 8:6)

APPENDIX

BAYES'S THEOREM

Probable evidence, in its very nature, affords but an imperfect kind of information; and is to be considered as relative only to beings of limited capacities. For nothing which is the possible object of knowledge, whether past, present, or future, can be probable to an infinite Intelligence; since it cannot but be discerned absolutely as it is in itself – certainly true, or certainly false. But to us, probability is the very guide of life.

Bishop Joseph Butler (1736)[1]

In Chapter 9 I introduced Bayes's theorem as a means of evaluating evidence for a hypothesis. I gave the examples of a diagnostic test and a witness to a crime, before going on to apply the same kind of reasoning to the central argument of this book, namely that the existence of our universe, with its ultra finely-tuned character, furnishes good evidence for the existence of God. For the more mathematically inclined reader, in this appendix I briefly summarize what the theorem says and how it can be so used.

If H is a hypothesis and E some piece of evidence, we use the notation $P[H]$ to mean the prior probability of H and $P[E|H]$ to mean the probability of finding E on the assumption that H is true, i.e. the likelihood of hypothesis H on evidence E. $P[E|H]$ is called a conditional probability and is read "probability of E given H". Then Bayes's theorem is a straightforward consequence of the axioms of probability theory. It states:

$$P[H|E] = \frac{P[E|H]P[H]}{P[E]}$$

The "total probability" rule enables us to expand the denominator in the above:

$$P[E] = P[E \mid H]P[H] + P[E \mid \sim H]P[\sim H]$$

where $\sim H$ means the negation of H, i.e. "H is not true."

Hence we can write:

$$P[H \mid E] = \frac{P[E \mid H]P[H]}{P[E \mid H]P[H] + P[E \mid \sim H]P[\sim H]} \quad (1)$$

In fact, all the probabilities defined so far should also be conditioned on background knowledge; that is, knowledge taken for granted in any application, such as the rules of logic and tautologies. I have omitted this modification for the sake of simplicity.

Now consider the diagnostic test example from Chapter 9. Let E = "the test is positive" and let H = "I have the disease." Then, putting in the numbers from Chapter 9, we obtain $P[H]$ = 0.01, $P[E|H]$ = 0.9, $P[E|\sim H]$ = 0.1. Since $P[\sim H]$ = 1 – $P[H]$ = 0.99, it follows from (1) that

$$P[H \mid E] = \frac{0.9 \times 0.01}{0.9 \times 0.01 + 0.1 \times 0.99} = \frac{1}{12}$$

as stated in the main text.

Now consider the second example in Chapter 9, the reporting of a hit-and-run accident. Let E = "the witness reports seeing a blue taxi" and let H = "the car which left the victim behind *was* a blue taxi." Then, again putting in the numbers from Chapter 9, we obtain $P[H]$ = 1 – 0.85 = 0.15, $P[E|H]$ = 0.8, $P[E|\sim H]$ = 0.2. Since $P[\sim H]$ = 0.85, it follows from (1) that

$$P[H \mid E] = \frac{0.8 \times 0.15}{0.8 \times 0.15 + 0.2 \times 0.85} \approx 0.41,$$

again, as stated in the text.

Suppose we want to compare two hypotheses H_1 and H_2 as possible explanations for evidence E. Bayes's theorem gives:

$$P[H_1 \mid E] = \frac{P[E \mid H_1]P[H_1]}{P[E]} \text{ and } P[H_2 \mid E] = \frac{P[E \mid H_2]P[H_2]}{P[E]}$$

By dividing these two expressions we obtain the very useful formula

$$\frac{P[H_1 \mid E]}{P[H_2 \mid E]} = \frac{P[E \mid H_1]}{P[E \mid H_2]} \cdot \frac{P[H_1]}{P[H_2]}$$

That is to say, the ratio of the posterior probabilities of the hypotheses is the product of the ratio of the likelihoods and the ratio of the prior probabilities. For the diagnostic test, putting in the numbers yields:

$$\frac{P[H \mid E]}{P[\sim H \mid E]} = \frac{P[E \mid H]}{P[E \mid \sim H]} \cdot \frac{P[H]}{P[\sim H]} = \frac{0.9}{0.1} \cdot \frac{0.01}{0.99} = \frac{1}{11}$$

i.e. I am eleven times more likely not to have the disease than to have it. Another way of expressing the result is to say that the odds are eleven to one against me having it.

Let us now consider the evidence E to be the fine-tuning and let us compare the hypothesis G that there is a God with the hypothesis M that there is a multiverse, say the string theory landscape version of the multiverse, but no God. Then we have:

$$\frac{P[G \mid E]}{P[M \mid E]} = \frac{P[E \mid G]}{P[E \mid M]} \cdot \frac{P[G]}{P[M]} \qquad (2)$$

I argue in the main text of Chapter 10 that $P[G]$ should be taken to be much higher that $P[M]$, largely on the grounds that God is a much simpler hypothesis than a multiverse. As I have noted several times, for the multiverse there is always the question, "Why this multiverse in particular?"

I have also argued that if one construes the evidence carefully then $P[E \mid G]$ should be very, very much larger than $P[E \mid M]$. Naïvely, a multiverse raises the probability that a fine-tuned universe exists, and a multiverse with the same laws as our universe but with all possible variations of the physical constants would ensure that a universe with our parameters exists. Besides certain difficulties with infinite numbers of universes, there is the very serious problem that although such a universe would exist, it is unlikely in the extreme that we should find ourselves as observers in it. The arguments of Penrose, Mawson, and Collins render that utterly improbable.

On the other hand, although God may not make precisely this universe, he is very likely to make a universe like ours, which is highly ordered, in which the principle of induction works, and in which we can do science and understand the world. Given a multiverse, we are far more likely to find ourselves as Boltzmann brains, or inhabiting a solar system surrounded by chaos, or in a universe in which induction breaks down, or in a universe that we can only understand in a limited way, than in the highly ordered universe in which we find ourselves. Thus $P[E|G]$ should far exceed $P[E|M]$ – on Penrose's calculation by the unimaginably enormous factor of $10^{10^{123}}$.

The upshot is that, on the argument of this book, both the ratio of the likelihoods in equation (2) and the ratio of the priors are large and positive, with the former being utterly astronomical. Even if the ratio of the priors is taken to be about one, as Paul Davies thinks it should be, the factor $10^{10^{123}}$ will utterly dominate and render the probability that God exists given the evidence vastly higher than the probability that an uncaused multiverse exists given the evidence.

It seems to me that the only way the atheist can avoid this conclusion is by arguing that the concept of God is incoherent or that God is necessarily impossible. If God is possible, then for the atheist the prior probability of God's existence has to be smaller than 1 in $10^{10^{123}}$, a position I think even the staunchest of atheists would find hard to justify.

GLOSSARY

Note that italicized items within definitions cross-refer to their own, separate entries.

Absorption lines Dark lines in the colour spectrum of light from a star or nebula caused by the absorption of light at certain frequencies by various chemical elements. For a receding object, these lines are shifted to the red end of the spectrum; for an approaching object, they are shifted to the blue. See *Doppler shift* and *redshift*.

Anthropic principle The seemingly innocuous statement that the properties of the universe we observe must be compatible with our own existence. Variants include the *weak*, *strong*, and *participatory anthropic principles* (*WAP*, *SAP*, and *PAP*).

Anti-matter For every ordinary particle of matter there exists a corresponding anti-particle with the same mass but opposite electric charge, e.g. the anti-particles of the electron and proton are the positron and anti-proton respectively.

Bayes's theorem A theorem from probability theory which enables one to calculate the probability that a hypothesis is true given certain evidence, and to compare competing hypotheses.

Big Bang The modern cosmological theory that the universe began in an intensely hot and highly compact state some 13.8 billion years ago from which it has since expanded to produce the structure – galaxies, stars, and planets – we observe today.

Big Crunch The highly compact end state of a *closed* finite-sized universe which expands from a *Big Bang* and then recontracts.

Boltzmann brains See *fluctuation observers*.

Branes In the context of the *ekpyrotic model* of the universe, a three-dimensional world embedded in a four-dimensional space. In this theory our universe is supposed to result from the collision of two branes moving in the hidden, fourth dimension.

Chaotic cosmology Cosmological model of Charles Misner which purported to show that the universe would evolve in the same way regardless of initial conditions.

Chaotic inflation Variant of the theory of *inflation* in which many parts of the universe inflate at different rates, giving rise to a *multiverse*.

Closed causal loops The paradoxical idea that we are both caused by past events and that we create the past. Proponents of this view justify it by appeal to the fact that in *quantum theory* a system is in a mixture of states, rather than a single definite state, until a measurement is made.

Closed universe A universe in which the *curvature of space* is positive. Such a universe will be finite in size, and space will "curve back on itself". An analogy in two dimensions is the surface of a sphere.

Conformal cyclic cosmology Speculative theory of Sir Roger Penrose in which the end state of an infinite *open* universe provides the beginning state for another similar *Big Bang*. This is in contrast to Penrose's demonstration that, for standard cosmological models, the end and beginning states are totally asymmetric.

Contingency Something is contingent (a) if its existence is possible but not necessary and/or (b) its properties could be different from what they are. Opposite to *necessity*.

Continuous creation (a) In cosmology the claim of steady-state theory that matter comes into existence in the space between the galaxies as the universe expands; (b) in theology the doctrine that God is creatively involved in upholding and sustaining the universe at every moment of its existence, and that it would collapse into nothing unless this were so. These two ideas are in fact compatible!

Cosmic background radiation Relic radiation suffusing the universe, stemming from the period about 380,000 years from the *Big Bang* when protons and electrons combined to form atoms and the universe became transparent to radiation. It has cooled from about 4000 K then to about 2.7 K now. (NB temperatures are in degrees above absolute zero: subtract 273 to get temperatures in degrees Celsius.)

Cosmological constant An extra term introduced by Einstein into his equations for the *general theory of relativity*, and set to a particular value in order to obtain a static universe. Now identified with *dark energy*.

Critical density Value of the mean density of matter–energy above which the *curvature of space* will be positive, below which it will be negative, and equal to which it will be zero (a so-called "flat" space).

Critical realism Philosophical position according to which the world is real – that is, not just a construct of our minds – and through our scientific theories we have imperfect but growing knowledge of that world.

Crossover point Point in the universe's history when matter and radiation have equal density. The early universe was radiation dominated; after the crossover point matter dominates.

Curvature of space According to Einstein's *general theory of relativity* space can be curved due to the presence of matter. The universe as a whole can be positively curved, negatively curved, or "flat" depending on whether the mean density of matter–energy is above, below or equal to the *critical density*. Two-dimensional analogies for these spaces are the surface of a sphere, a saddle shape, and a flat plane respectively.

Dark energy Energy associated with the *quantum vacuum* and giving rise to the *cosmological constant*.

Dark matter Unknown form of matter that is deemed to exist because of its gravitational pull on visible matter. Stars are orbiting their galaxies' centres too fast to be held by the gravity of the mass we can observe, so without dark matter galaxies would fly apart.

Density Quantity of matter–energy contained in a unit of volume. Cosmological models assume as an approximation that the universe is homogeneous (see *homogeneity*), meaning that the density is the same everywhere in the universe.

Density fluctuations Departures from total *homogeneity* in density, which were necessary in the early universe for structure to evolve.

Dimensionality of space We normally think of space as three dimensional. Any point in such a space can be specified using three numbers called coordinates. Mathematicians routinely study spaces, and corresponding coordinate systems, with other than three dimensions, and some cosmological models propose physical spaces of more than three dimensions.

Doppler shift The change in frequency of sound or light waves received from an object in motion. The frequency is higher for an approaching object and lower for a receding object. See also *redshift*.

Einstein–de Sitter model This is a cosmological model with zero *cosmological constant* in which the *density* of matter–energy is equal to the *critical density*, and thus the *curvature of space* is "flat".

Ekpyrotic model From the Greek ekpyrosis (ἐκπύρωσις) meaning conflagration or conversion into fire, this is an alternative model to *inflation* in which two three-dimensional *branes* moving in a fourth dimension collide to start our *Big Bang* universe.

Empiricism Philosophical position that our knowledge of the world comes solely or mainly from sensory experience (in contrast to rationalism, the exercise of pure reason). In science, this means that our knowledge comes from observational or experimental evidence. Modern philosophers of science speak of the "theory-ladenness of observation", meaning that pure empiricism needs to be tempered by the recognition that we always bring some prior theoretical framework to our observations and experiments.

Entropy A measure of the degree of "disorder" in a system. See *thermodynamics, second law of*.

Eternal inflation Further development of *chaotic inflation* in which some inflating regions produce subregions which inflate, these in turn produce sub-subregions which inflate, and so on. In other words, we have a *multiverse* in which universes spawn other universes, ad infinitum.

Fake universes Computer simulations of universes by advanced technological civilizations.

Fine-tuning This refers to the seemingly special way in which the initial conditions at the *Big Bang* and the constants which go into the laws of physics are arranged so that the universe gives rise to carbon-based life.

FLRW models Solutions of Einstein's equations for the *general theory of relativity* applied to the whole universe under certain simplifying assumptions, especially that the universe exhibits *homogeneity* and *isotropy*. FLRW stands for Friedmann–Lemaître–Robertson–Walker.

Fluctuation observers Entities that come into being through the localized random collisions of atoms and radiation, and possess just enough structure to have conscious experiences. Also called *Boltzmann brains*.

General theory of relativity Einstein's theory of gravity, according to which matter, space, and time are intimately connected: matter tells space–time how to curve and the curvature of space–time tells matter how to move.

Geodesic The shortest path between two points. In a flat plane this is a straight line, and parallel lines stay the same distance apart. A more counter-intuitive example would be the surface of the earth, where lines of longitude are parallel geodesics, which meet at the poles. The concept can be generalized to three-dimensional curved spaces.

Homogeneity The universe is homogeneous if it looks the same at all places within it, i.e. if matter is evenly distributed across it. The assumption of homogeneity provides a very useful approximation to the large-scale properties of the universe in cosmology.

Hoyle resonance Discovered by Sir Fred Hoyle, this is a particular value the energy in the carbon nucleus can take which ensures that carbon is produced in sufficient quantities in stars for the subsequent development of life. See also *triple-alpha process*.

Hubble's law States that the velocity of recession of distant nebulae is proportional to their distance.

Imaginary time In a theory of Stephen Hawking and Jim Hartle, as one approaches the origin of the universe at the *Big Bang* time becomes "imaginary" in the technical sense used by mathematicians. An imaginary number is a multiple of the square root of -1. This means that time is then just like a fourth space dimension.

Induction, principle of States that general laws can be inferred from particular instances, and relies on the future resembling the past.

Inflation Modification of the standard *Big Bang* model in which a period of enormously rapid expansion of the universe is postulated in the first 10^{-32} seconds from the origin.

Isotropy The universe is isotropic if it looks the same in all directions. Along with *homogeneity*, the assumption of isotropy gives a very useful approximation to the real universe, which enables us to find solutions to the equations of the *general theory of relativity* applied to the universe as a whole (the *FLRW models*).

***Kalām* cosmological argument** Originating in the medieval Islamic world, this goes as follows: (1) everything that begins to exist has a cause of its existence; (2) the universe began to exist; (3) therefore, the universe has a cause of its existence.

Landscape of string theory A *multiverse* version of *string theory* in which different universes represent different solutions of the theory.

Likelihood The likelihood of a hypothesis with respect to certain evidence is the probability that the evidence pertains if the hypothesis is true. Needed as an input into *Bayes's theorem*.

Many worlds interpretation of quantum theory *Multiverse* interpretation of *quantum theory* according to which all possible outcomes of a quantum measurement are realized but in different, parallel universes.

"Maximal multiverse" Concept of cosmologist Max Tegmark which deems all mathematical structures to have physical existence.

Model-dependent realism Philosophical position adopted by Stephen Hawking and Leonard Mlodinow according to which it is pointless to ask whether a model is real, only whether it agrees with observations.

M-theory Theory which unifies the original five versions of *string theory*.

Multiverse Ensemble of universes which are deemed to exist in reality rather than simply as possibilities. Cosmologists conceive multiple ways in which multiverses might be realized.

Necessary being A being who cannot but exist. An alternative way of expressing this is to say that a necessary being exists in all possible universes.

Necessity Expresses what must be the case, as opposed to mere possibility or *contingency*. Thus the laws of logic express necessary truths (they are true of necessity), and God is conceived to be a *necessary being*.

No boundary proposal Speculative theory of Stephen Hawking and Jim Hartle according to which, as one goes back towards the beginning of the universe at the *Big Bang*, space–time gets "smoothed out" and time becomes like a fourth space dimension (see *imaginary time*). Hawking argues that the universe then has no boundary or edge at which the laws of physics break down.

Observer selection effect The measurements we as observers make of the values of physical constants etc. are constrained by the fact that *we* are making them, i.e. we can only observe or measure values that are compatible with our own existence.

Observer selection principle Elevation of *observer selection effect* to the status of a principle. Observers can only exist in regions of space–time where the constants of physics etc. take values compatible with their existence.

Ockham's razor Principle for choosing among competing hypotheses on the basis of simplicity. Commonly stated as "Entities are not to be multiplied beyond necessity", though these precise words are not found in William of Ockham's extant works.

Open universe A universe in which the *curvature of space* is negative or zero. Such a universe will be infinite in size and parallel *geodesics* will diverge from one another. An analogy in two dimensions is a saddle shape.

Oscillating universes Universes in which successive *big bangs* are succeeded by *big crunches*, which are in turn succeeded by further big bangs and big crunches ad infinitum.

Participatory anthropic principle (PAP) Highly controversial and speculative claim that "Observers are necessary to bring the universe into being" (Barrow and Tipler, following Wheeler).

Perfect cosmological principle
Principle of Bondi and Gold that
"apart from local irregularities the
universe presents the same aspect from
any place at any time."

Posterior probability Probability of a
hypothesis revised to take into account
specific evidence. Calculated from
Bayes's theorem.

Primeval atom Cosmological model
of Georges Lemaître, according to
which the universe begins as a single,
highly compact quantum of energy a
finite time in the past. As developed by
George Gamow and others, we now
know this as the *Big Bang* model.

Prior probability Probability of a
hypothesis before specific evidence
is taken into account. Needed as an
input into *Bayes's theorem*.

Proton–electron mass ratio Protons
and electrons are particles with equal
but opposite charge: protons are
positively charged and electrons are
negatively charged. In atoms, protons
are constituents of the nucleus and
electrons are grouped in shells around
the nucleus. The ratio of the mass of a
proton to that of an electron is 1,837.

Quantum theory Counter-intuitive
physical theory required to explain
phenomena at the very small scale of
atoms. According to quantum theory
a physical system is not in a definite
state until a measurement is made.

Quantum vacuum In *quantum theory*
the vacuum is not empty but a sea of
activity in which particles and their
anti-particles are spontaneously created
and annihilated.

Radiation density Electromagnetic
radiation can be thought of as
discrete amounts or quanta of energy.
Radiation density is the energy of
radiation per unit volume and the
most important contributor to the
overall mass–energy *density* in the early
universe.

Redshift The shift in frequency
towards the red of *absorption lines*
in the spectrum of a distant galaxy
receding from us. An example of
Doppler shift.

Relativity, general theory of See
general theory of relativity.

Resonance When two atomic nuclei
combine to form a third, the reaction
is "resonant" and proceeds efficiently if
there is an energy level in the product
nucleus lying just below the total
energy, including energy of motion, of
the two combining nuclei. See *Hoyle
resonance*.

Simplicity Criterion of theory choice:
one hypothesis is said to be simpler
than another, and therefore more
likely to be true, if it postulates fewer
entities and kinds of entities than the
alternative. See also *Ockham's razor*.

Singularity Point of infinite density at
which the laws of physics break down.
Found at the centre of a black hole
and at the origin of the universe in the
Big Bang.

Steady-state theory Alternative to the
Big Bang. As the universe expands,
the continuous creation of matter at
the right rate in the space between
the galaxies ensures that the universe
looks the same at all times and in all
places, in accordance with the *perfect
cosmological principle*.

String theory The theory that
attempts to unite *quantum theory* and

gravity by postulating that matter consists of "strings", one-dimensional objects whose vibrations give rise to the different species of elementary particle.

Strong anthropic principle (SAP) Controversial claim that "The Universe must have those properties which allow life to develop within it at some stage in its history" (Barrow and Tipler, following Brandon Carter).

Theory of everything (TOE) Theory sought by physicists to unite all four fundamental forces of nature, and in particular to unite the *general theory of relativity* and *quantum theory* in a consistent way. The chief contenders are *string theory* or the more general *M-theory*.

Thermodynamics, second law of States that the *entropy*, or disorder, of an isolated system will increase with time. This is essentially because there are more disordered states than ordered ones.

Triple-alpha reaction An alpha particle is a helium nucleus, so this is the combining of three helium nuclei to form carbon via the intermediate, unstable element beryllium. See also *Hoyle resonance*.

Weak anthropic principle (WAP) The uncontroversial claim that "What we can expect to observe must be restricted by the conditions necessary for our presence as observers" (Brandon Carter). Equivalent to *observer selection principle*.

NOTES

Foreword

1. Scientists conventionally use American billions, so one billion is one thousand million.

1. The Big Bang: History of a Scientific Theory

1. Georges Lemaître, *The Primeval Atom: An Essay on Cosmogony*, trans. Betty H. and Serge A. Korff (New York, Toronto, London: D. Van Nostrand, 1950), 78.

2. Helge Kragh, *Cosmology and Controversy* (Princeton, NJ: Princeton University Press, 1996), 10.

3. George Smoot and Keay Davidson, *Wrinkles in Time: The Imprint of Creation* (London: Little, Brown and Company, 1993), 54; Kragh, *Cosmology and Controversy*, 30.

4. A. S. Eddington, "On the Instability of Einstein's Spherical World", *Monthly Notices of the Royal Astronomical Society* 90 (1930): 668–78.

5. G. Lemaître, "A Homogeneous Universe of Constant Mass and Increasing Radius", *Monthly Notices of the Royal Astronomical Society* 91 (1931): 483–90.

6. G. Lemaître, "The Beginning of the World from the Point of View of Quantum Theory", *Nature* 127 (1931): 706.

7. Quoted in Kragh, *Cosmology and Controversy*, 50.

8. G. Lemaître, "L'expansion de l'espace", *Revue des Questions Scientifiques* 17 (1931), 391–440.

9. John Farrell, *The Day Without Yesterday: Lemaître, Einstein, and the Birth of Modern Cosmology* (New York: Thunder's Mouth Press, 2005), 225–26, n. 73.

10. Kragh. *Cosmology and Controversy*, 54; also cited in Farrell, *Day Without Yesterday*, 169. There is a facsimile of the letter in Farrell, *Day Without Yesterday*, 143.

11. This section contains material adapted from Rodney Holder, "Georges Lemaître and Fred Hoyle: Contrasting Characters in Science and Religion", in *Georges Lemaître: Life, Science and Legacy*, ed. Rodney D. Holder and Simon Mitton (Heidelberg: Springer, 2012), 39–53.

12. When we say that the three-digit number 13.8 is accurate to three significant figures we mean that it lies between 13.75 and 13.85.

13. Arthur Eddington, "The End of the World: from the Standpoint of Mathematical Physics", *Nature* 127 (1931): 447–53; quoted in Kragh, *Cosmology and Controversy*, 46.

14. Kragh, *Cosmology and Controversy*, 76.

15. Kragh, *Cosmology and Controversy*, 142.

16. Hermann Bondi, *Cosmology* (Cambridge: Cambridge University Press, 1961), 12.

17. Kragh, *Cosmology and Controversy*, 150.

18. Peter J. Bowler, *Reconciling Science and Religion: The Debate in Early-Twentieth-Century Britain* (Chicago and London: Chicago University Press, 2001), 270–77.

19. E. L. Mascall, *Christian Theology and Natural Science* (London: Longmans, Green

and Co., 1956), 158–59, quoting Aquinas's *Summa Theologiae*, I.9.2.

20. Kragh, *Cosmology and Controversy*, 174.

21. Hoyle, quoted in Kragh, *Cosmology and Controversy*, 179.

22. Kragh, *Cosmology and Controversy*, 275.

23. Kragh, *Cosmology and Controversy*, 177.

24. Kragh, *Cosmology and Controversy*, 182.

25. Bondi, *Cosmology*, 143.

26. Fred Hoyle, *The Nature of the Universe* (Oxford: Blackwell, 1950), 106.

27. The formula is $N \propto S^{-3/2}$ where N is the number of sources of brightness greater than S. It follows from this that $\log N = -3/2 \log S +$ constant, so a plot of $\log N$ against $\log S$ should yield a straight line of slope $-3/2$. It is relatively easy to verify such a straight line law.

2. The Big Bang Triumphs

1. Interview of George Gamow by Charles Weiner on 25 April 1968, Niels Bohr Library & Archives, American Institute of Physics, College Park, MD USA, <http://www.aip.org/history/ohilist/4325.html>, accessed 26 March 2013. The third and fourth verses are quoted in Helge Kragh, "Big Bang: The Etymology of a Name", *A&G: News and Reviews in Astronomy and Geophysics* 54, no. 2 (2013): 28–30 (30).

2. This and the next section contain material adapted from Rodney Holder, "Georges Lemaître and Fred Hoyle: Contrasting Characters in Science and Religion", in *Georges Lemaître: Life, Science and Legacy*, ed. Rodney D. Holder and Simon Mitton (Heidelberg: Springer, 2012), 39–53.

3. Helge Kragh, *Cosmology and Controversy* (Princeton, NJ: Princeton University Press, 1996), 28.

4. Kragh, *Cosmology and Controversy*, 226.

5. Kragh, *Cosmology and Controversy*, 195.

6. Kragh, *Cosmology and Controversy*, 238.

7. Kragh, *Cosmology and Controversy*, 253.

8. Fred Hoyle, *Frontiers of Astronomy* (London: Heinemann, 1970 [1955]), 353–55.

9. Fred Hoyle, *The Nature of the Universe* (Oxford: Blackwell, 1950), 105.

10. Kragh, "Big Bang: Etymology of a Name".

11. Hoyle, *Nature of the Universe*, 115–16.

12. Simon Mitton, *Fred Hoyle: A Life in Science* (London: Aurum Press, 2005), 172.

13. Mitton, *Fred Hoyle*, 135–37.

14. Kragh, *Cosmology and Controversy*, 395.

15. Foreword by Paul Davies to Mitton, *Fred Hoyle*, x.

16. Hoyle, *Frontiers of Astronomy*, 351.

17. Fred Hoyle, in *Religion and the Scientists*, ed. Mervyn Stockwood (London: SCM Press, 1959), 57–58.

18. Fred Hoyle, *Man and Materialism* (London: George Allen and Unwin, 1957), 139.

19. Hoyle, *Man and Materialism*, 157.

20. Hoyle, *Man and Materialism*, 152.

21. Hoyle, *Man and Materialism*, 152.

22. Hoyle, in *Religion and the Scientists*, 58.

23. Hoyle, in *Religion and the Scientists*, 56; Hoyle, *Man and Materialism*, 157.

24. Hoyle, *Man and Materialism*, 158.

25. Fred Hoyle, *Ten Faces of the Universe* (London: W. H. Freeman & Co., 1977).

26. Hoyle, *Ten Faces of the Universe*, 4.

27. Hoyle, *Ten Faces of the Universe*, 4, 6–7.

28. Hoyle, *Ten Faces of the Universe*, 7.

29. Hoyle, in *Religion and the Scientists*, 64.

30. Fred Hoyle, "The Universe: Some Past and Present Reflections", *Engineering & Science* (November 1981): 8–12 (12).

31. Hoyle, in *Religion and the Scientists*, 64.

32. Hoyle, "The Universe: Some Past and Present Reflections", 12.

33. Hoyle, *The Intelligent Universe* (London: Michael Joseph, 1983), 239.

34. Hoyle, *Intelligent Universe*, 237.

35. Odon Godart, "The Scientific Work of Georges Lemaître", in *The Big Bang and Georges Lemaître: Proceedings of a Symposium in Honour of G. Lemaître Fifty Years after his Initiation of Big-Bang Cosmology, Louvain-la-Neuve, Belgium, 10–13 October 1983*, ed. A. Berger (Dordrecht: Reidel, 1984), 395.

36. Kragh, *Cosmology and Controversy*, 198.

37. Kragh, *Cosmology and Controversy*, 60.

38. For more details, see Dominique Lambert, "Georges Lemaître: the Priest Who Invented the Big Bang", in *Georges Lemaître: Life, Science and Legacy*, ed. Rodney D. Holder and Simon Mitton, 9–21; and George V. Coyne, "Lemaître: Science and Religion", in *Georges Lemaître: Life, Science and Legacy*, 69–74.

39. Kragh, *Cosmology and Controversy*, 257.

40. Ernan McMullin, "How Should Cosmology Relate to Theology?" in *The Sciences and Theology in the Twentieth Century*, ed. Arthur Peacocke (Stocksfield: Oriel Press, 1981), 17–57; quoted in Kragh, *Cosmology and Controversy*, 431, n. 186.

41. George Gamow, *The Creation of the Universe* (New York: Viking Press, 1952); cited in E. L. Mascall, *Christian Theology and Natural Science* (London: Longmans, Green & Co., 1956), 153–54.

42. André Deprit, "Monsignor Georges Lemaître", in *The Big Bang and Georges Lemaître*, ed. A. Berger, 387.

43. Simon Singh, *Big Bang: The most important scientific discovery of all time and why you need to know about it* (London: Fourth Estate, 2004), 157.

44. Kragh, *Cosmology and Controversy*, 59.

45. John Farrell, *The Day Without Yesterday: Lemaître, Einstein, and the Birth of Modern Cosmology* (New York: Thunder's Mouth Press, 2005), 191.

46. Farrell, *Day Without Yesterday*, 156–57.

47. Kragh, *Cosmology and Controversy*, 112–13.

48. Kragh, *Cosmology and Controversy*, 113.

49. Kragh, *Cosmology and Controversy*, 113.

50. Absolute zero is the theoretically lowest conceivable temperature, i.e. the lower limit which temperature can approach but not quite reach. It is –273 °C.

51. Kragh, *Cosmology and Controversy*, 120.

52. Kragh, *Cosmology and Controversy*, 127.

53. P. J. E. Peebles, "Primordial Helium Abundance and the Primordial Fireball, II", *Astrophysical Journal* 146 (1966): 542–52.

54. R. V. Wagoner, W. A. Fowler, and F. Hoyle, "On the Synthesis of Elements at Very High Temperatures", *Astrophysical Journal* 148 (1967): 3–49.

55. E. M. Burbidge, G. R. Burbidge, W. A. Fowler, and F. Hoyle, "Synthesis of the Elements in Stars", *Reviews of Modern Physics* 29 (1957): 547–650.

56. The letter is in the possession of St John's College Library, Cambridge, and may be viewed at <http://www.joh.cam.ac.uk/sites/default/files/images/article_images/hoyle-object03_big_0.jpg>.

57. I should add that nucleosynthesis of elements heavier than iron occurs when the most massive stars explode as supernovae.

58. Kragh, *Cosmology and Controversy*, 349.

59. Kragh, *Cosmology and Controversy*, 350.

60. Kragh, *Cosmology and Controversy*, 351.

61. Dennis Sciama, *Modern Cosmology* (Cambridge: Cambridge University Press, 1971), 181–84.

62. Kragh, *Cosmology and Controversy*, 345.

3. The Big Bang: Does a Beginning Require God?

1. William Cowper, *The Task: A Poem, in Six Books*, Book VI, "The Winter Walk at Noon" (1785), lines 221–30.

2. I was also invited to write the article on which some of what follows in the main text is based: see Rodney Holder (2011), "God and the Multiverse: A Response to Stephen Hawking", *Faith and Thought* 51 (2011): 3–17.

3. Stephen Hawking and Leonard Mlodinow, *The Grand Design: New Answers to the Ultimate Questions of Life* (London: Bantam Press, 2010).

4. Hawking and Mlodinow, *Grand Design*, 46.

5. Hawking and Mlodinow, *Grand Design*, 50.

6. Hawking and Mlodinow, *Grand Design*, 50–51.

7. Hawking and Mlodinow, *Grand Design*, 127.

8. Clement of Alexandria, *Stromata*, Book VI, ch. XVI (Gnostic Exposition of the Decalogue, *The Fourth Commandment*), in *Ante-Nicene Fathers*, vol. 2, ed. Alexander Roberts and James Donaldson (Peabody, MA: Hendrickson, 1994), 513.

9. Philo of Alexandria, "On the Creation", VII (26), in *The Works of Philo*, new updated edition, trans. C. D. Yonge (Peabody, MA: Hendrickson, 1993), 5.

10. St Augustine, *The City of God (De Civitate Dei)* XI.6, in *Nicene and Post-Nicene Fathers*, First Series, Vol. 2, ed. Philip Schaff (Peabody, MA: Hendrickson, 1994), 208.

11. St Augustine, *The Literal Meaning of Genesis (De Genesi ad Litteram)*, Ancient Christian Writers, vols 1 and 2, translated and annotated by John Hammond Taylor SJ (New York and Mahwah, NJ: Paulist Press, 1982), V, 5, 12, 153–54.

12. Augustine, *Literal Meaning of Genesis*, V, 5, 12, 154.

13. Augustine, *Literal Meaning of Genesis*, IV, 12, 22, 117.

14. William Lane Craig, *The Kalām Cosmological Argument* (London: Macmillan Press, 1979); see also the more recent Paul Copan and William Lane Craig, *Creation out of Nothing: A Biblical, Philosophical, and Scientific Exploration* (Grand Rapids, MI: Baker Academic and Leicester: Apollos, 2004).

15. Robert J. Spitzer, *New Proofs of the Existence of God: Contributions of Contemporary Physics and Philosophy* (Grand Rapids, MI and Cambridge, UK: Eerdmans, 2010).

16. Stephen Hawking, *A Brief History of Time* (London: Bantam, 1988), 136.

17. Hawking, *Brief History of Time*, 140–41.

18. Hawking and Mlodinow, *Grand Design*, 134, 180.

19. See the somewhat more technical discussion in Rodney D. Holder, *God, the Multiverse, and Everything: Modern Cosmology and the Argument from Design* (Aldershot and Burlington, VT: Ashgate, 2004), 60–61; and in Quentin Smith, "The Wave Function of a Godless Universe", in William Lane Craig and Quentin Smith, *Theism, Atheism, and Big Bang Cosmology* (Oxford: Oxford University Press, 1993), 301–37 (315–21).

20. Quentin Smith, "Wave Function of a Godless Universe", 322.

21. Arvind Borde and Alexander Vilenkin, "Eternal Inflation and the Initial Singularity", *Physical Review Letters* 72, no. 21 (1994): 3305–08.

22. Arvind Borde, Alan H. Guth, and Alexander Vilenkin, "Inflationary Spacetimes Are Incomplete in Past Directions", *Physical Review Letters* 90, no. 15 (2003): 151301–1 – 151301–4.

23. Lisa Grossman, "Death of the Eternal Cosmos", *New Scientist* 213, no. 2847 (January 2012): 6–7.

24. Grossman, "Death of the Eternal Cosmos", 7.

25. Peter J. Bussey, "God as First Cause – a Review of the Kalām Argument", *Science and Christian Belief* 25, no. 1 (2013): 17–35.

4. The Christian Doctrine of Creation

1. Christopher Smart, "Song to David", in *The Oxford Book of English Verse 1250–1918*, ed. Sir Arthur Quiller-Couch, new edition (Oxford: Oxford University Press, 1983 [1939]), 554.

2. Origen, *On First Principles (De Principiis)* (Gloucester, MA: Peter Smith, 1973), IV, III, 1, 288.

3. St Augustine, *The Literal Meaning of Genesis (De Genesi ad Litteram)*, Ancient Christian Writers, vols 1 and 2, translated and annotated by John Hammond Taylor SJ (New York and Mahwah, NJ: Paulist Press, 1982), I, 19, 39, 42–43.

4. Quoted in R. Hooykaas, *Religion and the Rise of Modern Science* (Edinburgh: Scottish Academic Press, 1972), 118.

5. See, for example, M. B. Foster, "The Christian Doctrine of Creation and the Rise of Modern Science", *Mind* 43, no. 172 (1934): 446–68.

6. Hermas, Book II, "Commandment First", in *Ante-Nicene Fathers*, vol. 2, ed. Alexander Roberts and James Donaldson (Peabody, MA: Hendrickson, 1994), 20.

7. Theophilus to Autolycus, Book II, ch. IV, in *Ante-Nicene Fathers*, vol. 2, 95.

8. Irenaeus, *Adversus Haereses*, IV.20.1, in *Ante-Nicene Fathers*, vol. 1, ed. Alexander Roberts and James Donaldson (Peabody, MA: Hendrickson, 1994), 487–88.

9. Lawrence M. Krauss, *A Universe from Nothing: Why There is Something Rather than Nothing* (New York: Simon and Shuster, 2012).

10. Lewis Carroll, *Through the Looking Glass*, Chapter 7, in *Alice's Adventures in Wonderland and Through the Looking Glass* (Harmondsworth, Middlesex: Penguin, 1962), 286–89.

11. Colin E. Gunton, *The Triune Creator: A Historical and Systematic Study* (Edinburgh: Edinburgh University Press, 1998), 79–92.

12. Janet Soskice, "*Creatio ex nihilo*: its Jewish and Christian Foundations", in *Creation and the God of Abraham*, ed. David B. Burrell, Carlo Cogliati, Janet M. Soskice, and William R. Stoeger (Cambridge: Cambridge University Press, 2010), 24–39; William E. Carroll, "Aquinas and Contemporary Cosmology: Creation and Beginnings", in *Georges Lemaître: Life, Science and Legacy*, ed. Rodney D. Holder and Simon Mitton (Heidelberg: Springer, 2012), 75–88.

13. Augustine, *Literal Meaning of Genesis*, IV, 12, 23, 117.

14. St Thomas Aquinas, *Summa Theologiae*, 1a. 104, 1, Blackfriars Edition (London: Eyre and Spottiswoode, and New York: McGraw-Hill, 1974), 39.

15. *Summa Theologiae*, 1a. 46, 2.

16. *Summa Theologiae*, 1a. 2, 3.

17. Dietrich Bonhoeffer, *Letters and Papers from Prison*, The Enlarged Edition, ed. Eberhard Bethge (London: SCM Press, 1971), 359–60.

18. Bonhoeffer, *Letters and Papers*, 311–12.

19. I explore the thought of Bonhoeffer on science and religion in more detail in Rodney Holder, *The Heavens Declare: Natural Theology and the Legacy of Karl Barth* (West Conshohocken, PA: Templeton Press, 2012), 55–98.

20. Stephen Hawking and Leonard Mlodinow, *The Grand Design: New Answers to the Ultimate Questions of Life* (London: Bantam Press, 2010), 82, 140.

21. See the discussion in Roger P. Paul, "Relative State and It-from-Bit: God and Contrasting Interpretations of Quantum Theory", *Science and Christian Belief* 17, no. 2 (2005): 155–75; and Rodney D. Holder, "God and Differing Interpretations of Quantum Theory – Response to Paul", *Science and Christian Belief* 17, no. 2 (2005): 177–85.

22. In Paul Davies, *The Goldilocks Enigma: Why is the Universe Just Right for Life?* (London: Allen Lane, 2006), ch. 10.

23. Rodney Holder, "Quantum Theory and Theology", in *The Blackwell Companion to Science and Religion*, ed. J. B. Stump and Alan G. Padgett (Oxford: Wiley-Blackwell, 2012), 220–30.

24. John D. Barrow and Frank J. Tipler, *The Anthropic Cosmological Principle* (Oxford: Oxford University Press, 1986), 470–71.

25. Mary Midgley, *Science as Salvation: A Modern Myth and its Meaning* (London and New York: Routledge, 1992), 206–11.

26. Hawking and Mlodinow, *Grand Design*, 8–9.

27. Keith Ward, *God, Chance and Necessity* (Oxford: Oneworld, 1996), 34–49.

28. Hawking and Mlodinow, *Grand Design*, 29.

29. Stephen Hawking, *A Brief History of Time* (London: Bantam, 1988), 174.

30. Martin Rees, *Our Cosmic Habitat* (London: Weidenfeld and Nicolson, 2002), xi.

31. Helge Kragh, *Cosmology and Controversy* (Princeton, NJ: Princeton University Press, 1996), xi.

5. The Goldilocks Enigma

1. Sir James Jeans, *The Mysterious Universe* (Cambridge: Cambridge University Press, 1937 [1930]), 7.

2. John D. Barrow and Frank J. Tipler, *The Anthropic Cosmological Principle* (Oxford: Oxford University Press, 1986), 16.

3. Barrow and Tipler, *Anthropic Cosmological Principle*, 21.

4. For more technical discussion, see Rodney D. Holder, *God, the Multiverse, and Everything: Modern Cosmology and the Argument from Design* (Aldershot and Burlington, VT: Ashgate, 2004), 33–39.

5. D. J. Raine and E. G. Thomas, *An Introduction to the Science of Cosmology* (Bristol: Institute of Physics Publishing, 2001), 136.

6. Barrow and Tipler, *Anthropic Cosmological Principle*, 384–85.

7. Barrow and Tipler, *Anthropic Cosmological Principle*, 384–85.

8. Bernard Carr, "Lemaître's Prescience: The Beginning and End of the Cosmos", in *Georges Lemaître: Life, Science and Legacy*, ed. Rodney D. Holder and Simon Mitton (Heidelberg: Springer, 2012), 145–72 (152).

9. Carr, "Lemaître's Prescience", 153. The actual constraint is that the strength of the gravitational force is roughly equal to the strength of the weak nuclear force to the fourth power, i.e. to 10^{-40} in appropriate dimensionless units.

10. Barrow and Tipler, *Anthropic Cosmological Principle*, 305, citing T. Regge.

11. Roger Penrose, *The Emperor's New Mind: Concerning Computers, Minds, and the Laws of Physics* (Oxford: Oxford University Press, 1989), 343.

12. Rees, *Just Six Numbers: The Deep Forces that Shape the Universe* (London: Weidenfeld and Nicolson, 1999), 136; Stephen Hawking, *The Universe in a Nutshell* (London: Bantam, 2001), 88.

13. William Paley, *Natural Theology, or Evidence of the Existence and Attributes of the Deity, Collected from the Appearances of Nature* (Oxford: Oxford University Press, 2006 [1802]).

14. Quantitative expression was given to Paley's insight by physicist Paul Ehrenfest in a famous paper published in 1917 entitled "In What Way Does It Become Manifest in the Fundamental Laws of Physics That Space Has Three Dimensions?" See Barrow and Tipler, *Anthropic Cosmological Principle*, 260–62. Ehrenfest included the extension to atoms and molecules, and was able to be more rigorous in view of the recent advent of quantum theory.

15. See, for example, Barrow and Tipler, *Anthropic Cosmological Principle*, 417; Alan Guth, *The Inflationary Universe: The Quest for a New Theory of Cosmic Origins* (London: Jonathan Cape, 1997), 217.

16. This relationship is $\alpha_G \approx \alpha^{12} (m_e/m_p)^4$ where α_G is the strength of the gravitational force and α that of the electromagnetic force, both in natural non-dimensional units; m_e is the mass of the electron and m_p is the mass of the proton. The left-hand side of this equation $\approx 5.906 \times 10^{-39}$ whereas the right-hand side $\approx 2.2 \times 10^{-39}$. See Paul Davies, *The Accidental Universe* (Cambridge: Cambridge University Press, 1982), 71–73.

17. Davies, *Accidental Universe*, 73; the original argument is due to Brandon Carter and is in Brandon Carter, "Large Number Coincidences and the Anthropic Principle in Cosmology", in *Confrontation of Cosmological Theory with Astronomical Data*, ed. M. S. Longair (Dordrecht: Reidel, 1974), 291–98 (296–98).

18. Davies, *Accidental Universe*, 73.

19. Robin Collins, "Evidence for Fine-Tuning", in *God and Design: The Teleological Argument and Modern Science*, ed. Neil A. Manson (Abingdon: Routledge, 2003), 178–99 (189–90).

20. Rees, *Just Six Numbers*, 30–31.

21. John Leslie, *Universes* (London and New York: Routledge, 1989).

22. Alister E. McGrath, *A Fine-Tuned Universe: The Quest for God in Science and*

Theology (Louisville, KY: Westminster John Knox Press, 2009), 145–46.

23. Paul Davies, *The Goldilocks Enigma: Why is the Universe Just Right for Life?* (London: Allen Lane, 2006), 3.

6. Explaining the Fine-Tuning

1. Albert Einstein, letter to Maurice Solovine, 30 March 1952, quoted in Stanley Jaki, "Theological Aspects of Creative Science", in *Creation, Christ and Culture: Studies in Honour of T. F. Torrance*, ed. Richard W. A. McKinney (Edinburgh: T. and T. Clark, 1976), 164.

2. For more technical discussion of these issues, see Rodney D. Holder, *God, the Multiverse, and Everything: Modern Cosmology and the Argument from Design* (Aldershot and Burlington, VT: Ashgate, 2004), 9–10, 43–47.

3. Richard Feynman, *Six Easy Pieces: The Fundamentals of Physics Explained* (London: Penguin Books, 1995), xix.

4. Richard Swinburne, *The Existence of God*, second edition (Oxford: Oxford University Press, 2004), 156–57.

5. John Leslie, *Universes* (London and New York: Routledge, 1989), 13–14.

6. Paul Davies, *The Mind of God* (London: Simon and Schuster, 1992), 214.

7. Ernan McMullin, "Indifference Principle and Anthropic Principle in Cosmology", *Studies in History and Philosophy of Science* 24, no. 3 (1993): 359–89.

8. Peter van Inwagen, *Metaphysics* (Boulder, CO: Westview Press, 1993), 137–38.

9. Victor Stenger, *The Fallacy of Fine-Tuning: Why the Universe Is Not Designed for Us* (New York: Prometheus Books, 2011).

10. Luke Barnes, "The Fine-Tuning of the Universe for Intelligent Life", <http://arxiv.org/pdf/1112.4647v2.pdf>, accessed 25 September 2012.

11. Robin Collins, "Stenger's Fallacies", www.home.messiah.edu/~rcollins/Fine-tuning/Stenger-fallacy.pdf, accessed 12 August 2013.

12. H. Oberhummer, R. Pichler, and A. Csótó, "Fine-Tuning Carbon-Based Life in the Universe by the Triple-Alpha Process in Red Giants", <http://arxiv.org/pdf/astro-ph/9908247.pdf> (23 August 1999), accessed 2 October 2012. The result has been confirmed by Ekström *et al.*, who go further and translate this finding into a constraint on the electromagnetic force (electromagnetic fine-structure constant) of about 1 part in 10^5: see S. Ekström, A. Coc, P. Descouvement, G. Meynet, K. A. Olive, J.-P. Uzan, and E. Vangioni, "Effects of the Variation of Fundamental Constants on Population III Stellar Evolution", *Astronomy and Astrophysics* 514 (2010): A62.

13. Stenger, *Fallacy of Fine-Tuning*, 70.

14. S. M. Barr and A. Khan, "Anthropic Tuning of the Weak Scale and of m_u/m_d in Two-Higgs-Doublet Models", *Physical Review D*, 76 (2007): 045002.

15. M. Tegmark, A. Aguirre, M. J. Rees, and R. Wilczek, "Dimensionless Constants, Cosmology, and Other Dark Matters", *Physical Review D*, 73 (2006): 023505.

16. Max Tegmark, "Is 'The Theory of Everything' Merely the Ultimate Ensemble Theory?" *Annals of Physics* 270 (1998): 1–51 (24–40).

17. Max Tegmark, "Parallel Universes", *Scientific American* (May 2003), 30–41.

18. See the careful analysis in W. R. Stoeger, G. F. R. Ellis, and U. Kirchner, "Multiverses and Cosmology: Philosophical Issues", <http://arxiv.org/pdf/astro-ph/0407329.pdf> ([2004], v2 19 Jan 2006).

19. E.g. Ian Hacking, "The Inverse Gambler's Fallacy: the Argument from Design. The Anthropic Principle Applied to Wheeler Universes", *Mind* 96 (1987): 331–40; Roger White, "Fine-Tuning and Multiple Universes", *Noûs* 34, no. 2 (2000): 260–76.

20. My own more technical refutation of the theses of Hacking and White is given in Rodney D. Holder, "Fine-Tuning, Multiple Universes and Theism", *Noûs* 36, no. 2 (2002), 295–312, and also in Holder, *God, the Multiverse, and Everything*, 88-112.

7. Of the Making of Many Universes there is no End

1. St Albertus Magnus (*c.* AD 1260), *De Caelo et Mundo*, Lib. I, Tract III, Cap. I (*Opera*, Lugduni, 1651, II, 40), quoted in G. McColley, "The Seventeenth-Century Doctrine of a Plurality of Worlds", *Annals of Science* 1, no. 4 (1936): 385–430 (385).

2. C. W. Misner, "The Isotropy of the Universe", *Astrophysical Journal* 151 (1968): 431–57.

3. E. McMullin, "Indifference Principle and Anthropic Principle in Cosmology", *Studies in History and Philosophy of Science* 24, no. 3 (1993): 359–89.

4. S. W. Hawking and C. B. Collins, "Why is the Universe Isotropic?" *Astrophysical Journal* 180 (1973): 317–34.

5. Strictly speaking, the set of universes that become isotropic is "of measure zero". "Measure" is a technical mathematical way of quantifying the size of a set. Probability is defined in terms of measure, but not uniquely. However, any reasonable way of deriving probability on the basis of Collins' and Hawking's finding would make it zero.

6. J. A. Wheeler, "Beyond the End of Time", in C. W. Misner, K. S. Thorne, and J. A. Wheeler, *Gravitation* (San Francisco: W. H. Freeman, 1973), ch. 44.

7. As noted some time ago by Paul Davies. See P. C. W. Davies, *The Accidental Universe* (Cambridge: Cambridge University Press, 1982), 125.

8. Alan H. Guth, *The Inflationary Universe: The Quest for a New Theory of Cosmic Origins* (London: Jonathan Cape, 1997).

9. E. P. S. Shellard, "The Future of Cosmology: Observational and Computational Prospects", in *The Future of Theoretical Physics and Cosmology: Celebrating Stephen Hawking's 60th Birthday*, ed. G. W. Gibbons, E. P. S. Shellard, and S. J. Rankin (Cambridge: Cambridge University Press, 2003), 755–80 (764).

10. Leonard Susskind, *The Cosmic Landscape: String Theory and the Illusion of Intelligent Design* (New York: Little Brown and Company, 2006).

11. S. Kachru, R. Kallosh, A. Linde, and S. P. Trivedi, "de Sitter Vacua in String Theory", <http://arxiv.org/pdf/hep-th/0301240v2.pdf> (10 Feb 2003). See, however, the non-technical treatment in Susskind, *The Cosmic Landscape*.

12. Roger Penrose, *Cycles of Time: An Extraordinary New View of the Universe* (London: The Bodley Head, 2010).

13. Paul J. Steinhardt, "The Inflation Debate", *Scientific American* 304, no. 4 (2011): 36–43.

14. Roger Penrose, "Difficulties with Inflationary Cosmology", *Annals of the New York Academy of Sciences* 271 (1989): 249–64 (261).

15. Paul J. Steinhardt and Neil Turok, *Endless Universe: Beyond the Big Bang* (New York: Doubleday, 2007).

16. John Gribbin, *In Search of the Multiverse* (London: Allen Lane, 2009); for my review of this book, see Rodney Holder, review of John Gribbin, *In Search of the Multiverse*, in *Third Way* 33, no. 1 (Winter 2010): 39.

17. Brian Greene, *The Hidden Reality: Parallel Universes and the Deep Laws of the Cosmos* (London: Penguin, 2011), 8.

18. Wolfhart Pannenberg, *Towards a Theology of Nature: Essays on Science and Faith* (Louisville, KY: Westminster/John Knox Press, 1993), 100.

19. Pannenberg, *Towards a Theology of Nature*, 95.

20. I consider Pannenberg's thought on science and religion in Rodney Holder, *The Heavens Declare: Natural Theology and the Legacy of Karl Barth* (West Conshohocken, PA: Templeton Press, 2012), 99–138.

21. See, for example, A. R. Peacocke, *Theology for a Scientific Age*, second, enlarged edition (London: SCM Press, 1993), 107–09.

22. Robin Collins, "Evidence for Fine-Tuning", in *God and Design: The Teleological Argument and Modern Science*, ed. Neil Manson (London: Routledge, 2003), 178–99.

23. Robin Collins, "The Multiverse: A Theistic Perspective", in *Universe or Multiverse?* ed. Bernard Carr (Cambridge: Cambridge University Press, 2007), 459–80.

24. Susskind, *Cosmic Landscape*, 122–30.

25. Robin Collins, "Modern Cosmology and Anthropic Fine-tuning: Three Approaches", in *Georges Lemaître: Life, Science and Legacy*, ed. Rodney Holder and Simon Mitton (Heidelberg: Springer, 2012), 173–91.

26. E.g. Don N. Page, "Predictions and Tests of Multiverse Theories", in *Universe or Multiverse?* ed. Bernard Carr, 411–30; Don N. Page, "Multiple Reasons for a Multiverse", in *Georges Lemaître: Life, Science and Legacy*, ed. Rodney Holder and Simon Mitton (Heidelberg: Springer, 2012), 113–23.

27. Keith Ward, *The Big Questions in Science and Religion* (West Conshohocken, PA: Templeton Foundation Press, 2008), 233–35.

8. Multiple Problems for Multiverses

1. Giuseppe di Lampedusa, *The Leopard*, trans. Archibald Colquhoun, revised

edition (London: Collins & Harvill Press, 1961; first published as *Il Gattopardo* [Milan: Feltrinelli Editore, 1958]), 163.

2. A more technical treatment of some of these topics is to be found in Rodney D. Holder, *God, the Multiverse, and Everything: Modern Cosmology and the Argument from Design* (Aldershot and Burlington, VT: Ashgate, 2004), 113–29.

3. R. Feynman, in *Superstrings: A Theory of Everything?*, ed. P. C. W. Davies and J. Brown (Cambridge: Cambridge University Press, 1988), 194.

4. G. L. Kane, M. J. Perry, and A. N. Zytkow, "The Beginning of the End of the Anthropic Principle", <http://arxiv.org/pdf/astro-ph/0001197v2.pdf> (28 January 2000).

5. Peter Woit, *Not Even Wrong: The Failure of String Theory and the Continuing Challenge to Unify the Laws of Physics* (London: Jonathan Cape, 2006).

6. Lee Smolin, *The Trouble with Physics: The Rise of String Theory, the Fall of a Science and What Comes Next* (London: Allen Lane, 2006).

7. For an example of a landscape doubter, see T. Banks, "Landskepticism *or* Why Effective Potentials Don't Count String Models", <http://arxiv.org/pdf/hep-th/0412129v1.pdf> (13 December 2004).

8. Martin Rees, *New Perspectives in Astrophysical Cosmology*, second edition (Cambridge: Cambridge University Press, 2000), 138.

9. Rees, *New Perspectives*, 137–38.

10. Martin Rees, *Our Cosmic Habitat* (London: Weidenfeld & Nicolson, 2001), 164.

11. Leonard Susskind, *The Cosmic Landscape: String Theory and the Illusion of Intelligent Design* (New York: Little, Brown and Company, 2006), 380.

12. Susskind, *Cosmic Landscape*, 380.

13. See, especially, Jorge Luis Borges, "The Library of Babel", in *Labyrinths*, Penguin Classics Edition (London: Penguin, 2000), 78–86.

14. John Taylor, "Modern Cosmology and the Possibility of Causal Explanation of the Origins of the Universe", B. Phil. Thesis, University of Oxford (1995), 18–19.

15. G. F. R. Ellis and G. B. Brundrit, "Life in the Infinite Universe", *Quarterly Journal of the Royal Astronomical Society* 20 (1979): 37–41.

16. G. F. R. Ellis, U. Kirchner, and W. R. Stoeger, "Multiverses and Physical Cosmology", <http://arxiv.org/pdf/astro-ph/0305292v3.pdf> (28 August 2003). See also the twin philosophical paper, W. R. Stoeger, G. F. R. Ellis, and U. Kirchner, "Multiverses and Cosmology: Philosophical Issues", <http://arxiv.org/pdf/astro-ph/0407329v2.pdf> (16 July 2004).

17. T. J. Mawson, "Explaining the Fine Tuning of the Universe to Us and the Fine Tuning of Us to the Universe", *Royal Institute of Philosophy Supplement* 68 (2011): 25–50.

18. Mawson, "Explaining the Fine Tuning".

19. E.g. M. R. Douglas, "Statistics of String Vacua", <http://arxiv.org/pdf/hep-ph/0401004v1.pdf> (1 January 2004).

20. See Banks, "Landskepticism". Bernard Carr also notes that the issue of whether the number of solutions is large enough, and the spacing between them sufficiently small, has not been resolved. See Bernard Carr, "Introduction and Overview", in *Universe or Multiverse?* ed. Bernard Carr, 3–28 (6).

21. Banks, "Landskepticism".

22. Steven Weinberg, "Living in the Multiverse", in *Universe or Multiverse?* ed. Bernard Carr (Cambridge: Cambridge University Press, 2007), 29–42 (32).

23. Paul Davies, "Universes Galore: Where Will it all End?" in *Universe or Multiverse?* ed. Bernard Carr, 487–505 (492).

24. See Chapter 7, note 5, on "measure".

25. Leonard Susskind, "The Anthropic Landscape of String Theory", <http://arxiv.org/pdf/hep-th/0302219v1.pdf> (27 February 2003).

26. See J.-P. Luminet, J. Weeks, A. Riazuelo, R. Lehoucq, and J.-P. Uzan, "Dodecahedral Space Topology as an Explanation for Weak Wide-Angle Temperature Correlations in the Cosmic Microwave Background", <http://arxiv.org/pdf/astro-ph/0310253v1.pdf> (9 October 2003). A slightly edited version of this paper appeared in *Nature* 425 (9 October 2003): 593–95. A more popular, and somewhat updated, account is to be found in J.-P. Luminet, "A Cosmic Hall of Mirrors", *Physics World* 18, no. 9 (2005): 23–28.

27. Andrew H. Jaffe *et al.*, "*Planck* 2013 Results. XXVI. Background Geometry and Topology of the Universe", <http://arxiv.org/pdf/1303.5086v1.pdf> (20 March 2013).

28. John D. Barrow, *The Infinite Book* (London: Jonathan Cape, 2005), 144.

29. This example is discussed in Roger Penrose, *Cycles of Time: An Extraordinary New View of the Universe* (London: The Bodley Head, 2010), 16–19.

30. Penrose, *Cycles of Time*, 124.

31. Roger Penrose, *The Emperor's New Mind: Concerning Computers, Minds, and the Laws of Physics* (Oxford: Oxford University Press, 1989), 354.

32. Nick Bostrom, *Anthropic Bias: Observation Selection Effects in Science and Philosophy* (New York & London: Routledge, 2002).

33. Paul Davies, "Universes Galore", 492–93.

34. Frank Wilczek, "Enlightenment, Knowledge, Ignorance, Temptation", in *Universe or Multiverse?* ed. Bernard Carr, 43–54 (52).

35. Robin Collins, "Modern Cosmology and Anthropic Fine-tuning: Three Approaches", in *Georges Lemaître: Life, Science and Legacy*, ed. Rodney Holder and Simon Mitton (Heidelberg: Springer, 2012), 173–91.

36. *Notes Towards the Complete Works of Shakespeare* by Elmo, Gum, Heather, Holly, Mistletoe and Rowan, Sulawesi Crested Macaques (Macacanigra) from Paignton Zoo Environmental Park (UK), first published for vivaria.net in 2002; the experiment was carried out by students from the University of Plymouth's MediaLab Arts course.

37. Richard Dawkins, *The God Delusion* (London: Transworld, 2006), 159.

38. Paul Davies, "Universes Galore", 496.

39. Nick Bostrom, "Are We Living in a Computer Simulation?" *Philosophical Quarterly* 53, no. 211 (2003): 243–55.

40. Barrow, *Infinite Book*, 204.

41. Barrow, *Infinite Book*, 211.

9. Comparing the Explanations

1. Jorge Luis Borges, "The Library of Babel", in *Labyrinths: Selected Stories and Other Writings*, edited by Donald A. Yates and James E. Irby (London: Penguin Books, 1970 [original in Spanish, 1941]), 78–86 (82–83).

2. St Augustine, *The Literal Meaning of Genesis (De Genesi ad Litteram)*, Ancient Christian Writers, vol. 1, translated and annotated by John Hammond Taylor SJ (New York and Mahwah, NJ: Paulist Press, 1982), VI, 13, 23, 194.

3. For a valuable collection of essays on relationality in God and the physical world, see John Polkinghorne (ed.), *The Trinity and an Entangled World: Relationality in Physical Science and Theology* (Grand Rapids, MI, and Cambridge, UK: Wm B. Eerdmans, 2010).

4. Alvin Plantinga, *Where the Conflict Really Lies: Science, Religion, and Naturalism* (New York: Oxford University Press, 2011), 266–71.

5. Georges Lemaître, *The Primeval Atom: An Essay on Cosmogony*, trans. Betty H. and Serge A. Korff (New York, Toronto, London: D. Van Nostrand, 1950), 55.

6. Basil Mitchell, *The Justification of Religious Belief* (London: Macmillan, 1973); Richard Swinburne, *The Existence of God*, second edition (Oxford: Oxford University Press, 2004).

7. Of course, arguments on the other side should also be considered in a full appraisal, most notably the compatibility of the existence of pain and suffering with creation by a good God. Studies of this problem include, for example, John Hick, *Evil and the God of Love* (London: Macmillan, 1966); Richard Swinburne, *Providence and the Problem of Evil* (Oxford: Oxford University Press, 1998); and Brian Hebblethwaite, *Evil, Suffering, and Religion*, revised edition (London: SPCK, 2000).

8. Technical and philosophical discussion is given in Rodney D. Holder, *God, the Multiverse, and Everything: Modern Cosmology and the Argument from Design* (Aldershot and Burlington, VT: Ashgate, 2004), 69–87 161–63.

9. This example is adapted from one by Amos Tversky and Daniel Kahneman, and discussed in Ian Hacking, *An Introduction to Probability and Inductive Logic* (Cambridge: Cambridge University Press, 2001), 72–73.

10. Peter Donnelly, "Appealing Statistics", *Significance* 2, no. 1 (2005): 46–48.

11. See, for example, Peter Lipton, *Inference to the Best Explanation*, second edition (London: Routledge, 2004).

12. As we saw in Chapter 2, it would seem that metaphysical preferences impact both ways, e.g. Fred Hoyle preferred the steady state to the Big Bang because he thought the latter implied the need for a Creator,

and Pope Pius XII enthused about the Big Bang for the same reason. However, as we saw in Chapter 4, the essence of the theological doctrine of *creatio ex nihilo* is ontological, not temporal, dependence of the universe on God.

13. I explore some of these issues in Rodney D. Holder, "God and Differing Interpretations of Quantum Theory: Response to Paul", *Science and Christian Belief* 17, no. 2 (2005): 177–85.

10. Theism Wins

1. Albert Einstein (1955), in E. Salaman, "A Talk with Einstein", *The Listener* 54 (1955): 370–71; quoted in Max Jammer, *Einstein and Religion* (Princeton, NJ: Princeton University Press, 1999), 123.

2. Richard Swinburne, *The Existence of God*, second edition (Oxford: Oxford University Press, 2004), 54–55.

3. W. R. Stoeger, G. F. R. Ellis, and U. Kirchner, "Multiverses and Cosmology: Philosophical Issues", <http://arxiv.org/pdf/astro-ph/0407329v2.pdf> (16 July 2004).

4. Paul Davies, *The Goldilocks Enigma: Why is the Universe Just Right for Life?* (London: Allen Lane, 2006), 249.

5. Richard Dawkins, *The God Delusion* (London: Transworld, 2006), 137ff.

6. E.g. in Swinburne, *Existence of God*, 96–109.

7. William Lane Craig, "Design and the Anthropic Fine-Tuning of the Universe", in *God and Design*, ed. Neil A. Manson (London: Routledge, 2003), 155–77 (175).

8. Patrick Richmond, "Richard Dawkins' Darwinian Objection to Unexplained Complexity in God", *Science and Christian Belief* 19, no. 2 (2007): 99–116.

9. Eleonore Stump, review of Richard Swinburne, *The Existence of God*, first edition (Oxford: Oxford University Press, 1979), in *The Thomist* 46 (1982): 478–82.

10. Davies, *Goldilocks Enigma*, 231.

11. Keith Ward, *Religion and Creation* (Oxford: Oxford University Press, 1996), 186–91.

12. These issues are discussed in Rodney D. Holder, *God, the Multiverse, and Everything: Modern Cosmology and the Argument from Design* (Aldershot and Burlington, VT: Ashgate, 2004).

13. Keith Ward, *Why There Almost Certainly Is a God: Doubting Dawkins* (Oxford: Lion, 2008), 73.

14. Murphy makes the interesting proposal that theology should be treated as a "scientific research programme" utilizing the methodology of the great philosopher of science Imre Lakatos. See Nancey Murphy, *Theology in the Age of Scientific Reasoning* (Ithaca, NY, and London: Cornell University Press, 1990). As will be apparent, my preferred approach is that of Bayesian confirmation theory.

Appendix: Bayes's Theorem

1. Joseph Butler, Author's Introduction to *The Analogy of Religion Natural and Revealed* (London: J. M. Dent & Sons Ltd, 1906 [1736]), xxv.

FURTHER READING

Barrow, John D., *The Infinite Book* (London: Jonathan Cape, 2005).

Barrow, John D. and Tipler, Frank J., *The Anthropic Cosmological Principle* (Oxford: Oxford University Press, 1986).

Burrell, David B., Cogliati, Carlo, Soskice, Janet M., and Stoeger, William R. (eds), *Creation and the God of Abraham* (Cambridge: Cambridge University Press, 2010).

Carr, Bernard (ed.), *Universe or Multiverse?* (Cambridge: Cambridge University Press, 2007).

Copan, Paul and Craig, William Lane, *Creation out of Nothing: A Biblical, Philosophical, and Scientific Exploration* (Grand Rapids, MI: Baker Academic and Leicester: Apollos, 2004).

Craig, William Lane and Smith, Quentin, *Theism, Atheism, and Big Bang Cosmology* (Oxford: Oxford University Press, 1993).

Davies, Paul, *The Accidental Universe* (Cambridge: Cambridge University Press, 1982).

Davies, Paul, *The Goldilocks Enigma: Why is the Universe Just Right for Life?* (London: Allen Lane, 2006).

Farrell, John, *The Day Without Yesterday: Lemaître, Einstein, and the Birth of Modern Cosmology* (New York: Thunder's Mouth Press, 2005).

Gunton, Colin E., *The Triune Creator: A Historical and Systematic Study* (Edinburgh: Edinburgh University Press, 1998).

Guth, Alan H., *The Inflationary Universe: The Quest for a New Theory of Cosmic Origins* (London: Jonathan Cape, 1997).

Hawking, Stephen, *A Brief History of Time* (London: Bantam, 1988).

Hawking, Stephen and Mlodinow, Leonard, *The Grand Design: New Answers to the Ultimate Questions of Life* (London: Bantam Press, 2010).

Holder, Rodney D., *God, the Multiverse, and Everything: Modern Cosmology and the Argument from Design* (Aldershot and Burlington, VT: Ashgate, 2004).

Holder, Rodney D., *The Heavens Declare: Natural Theology and the Legacy of Karl Barth* (West Conshohocken, PA: Templeton Press, 2012).

Holder, Rodney D. and Mitton, Simon (eds), *Georges Lemaître: Life, Science and Legacy* (Heidelberg: Springer, 2012).

Kragh, Helge, *Cosmology and Controversy* (Princeton, NJ: Princeton University Press, 1996).

Krauss, Lawrence M., *A Universe from Nothing: Why There is Something Rather than Nothing* (New York: Simon and Schuster, 2012).

Lemaître, Georges, *The Primeval Atom: An Essay on Cosmogony*, trans. Betty H. and Serge A. Korff (New York, Toronto, London: D. Van Nostrand, 1950).

Leslie, John, *Universes* (London and New York: Routledge, 1989).

Manson, Neil (ed.), *God and Design: The Teleological Argument and Modern Science* (London: Routledge, 2003).

McGrath, Alister E., *A Fine-Tuned Universe: The Quest for God in Science and Theology* (Louisville, KY: Westminster John Knox Press, 2009).

Penrose, Roger, *The Emperor's New Mind: Concerning Computers, Minds, and the Laws of Physics* (Oxford: Oxford University Press, 1989).

Penrose, Roger, *Cycles of Time: An Extraordinary New View of the Universe* (London: The Bodley Head, 2010).

Rees, Martin, *Just Six Numbers: The Deep Forces that Shape the Universe* (London: Weidenfeld and Nicolson, 1999).

Rees, Martin, *Our Cosmic Habitat* (London: Weidenfeld and Nicolson, 2002).

Spitzer, Robert J., *New Proofs of the Existence of God: Contributions of Contemporary Physics and Philosophy* (Grand Rapids, MI and Cambridge, UK: Eerdmans, 2010).

Stenger, Victor, *The Fallacy of Fine-Tuning: Why the Universe Is Not Designed for Us* (New York: Prometheus Books, 2011).

Susskind, Leonard, *The Cosmic Landscape: String Theory and the Illusion of Intelligent Design* (New York: Little, Brown and Company, 2006).

Swinburne, Richard, *The Existence of God*, second edition (Oxford: Oxford University Press, 2004).

Ward, Keith, *God, Chance and Necessity* (Oxford: Oneworld, 1996).

Ward, Keith, *Religion and Creation* (Oxford: Oxford University Press, 1996).

Ward, Keith, *The Big Questions in Science and Religion* (West Conshohocken, PA: Templeton Foundation Press, 2008).

Ward, Keith, *Why There Almost Certainly Is a God: Doubting Dawkins* (Oxford: Lion, 2008).

Woit, Peter, *Not Even Wrong: The Failure of String Theory and the Continuing Challenge to Unify the Laws of Physics* (London: Jonathan Cape, 2006).

INDEX